Mothers and Daughters

Their Story, Their Way, Only They Can Tell It

By

Jacqueline Pitt

Aboe Banks

Alicia P. Harris

Carolyn Allen

Charlotte Cowser

Onita V. Simpson

Yashica B. Mack

ISBN: 978-0-578-87776-1

Published by Pamela Smalls Ball and SmallStories Publishing LLC.
Printed in the United States of America by Kindle Direct Publishing.

~ Table of Contents ~

~ Foreword ~

As a mother of daughters, I will always desire for them all the things that lead to a life of joy and love. A mother and daughter relationship can be complicated at times, and easy going at others.

I have watched many relationships between mothers and daughters over the years, in which some birthed some hard realities, and others, joy-filled moments. What I desired for my relationship with our daughters, is one that will bolster, and even if we did not agree on everything, we found a way to love through the differences. Unfortunately, I have known mothers and daughters that could not see their way through to the latter.

After observing and experiencing so much disconnect between this pivotal relationship, God placed it in my heart to bring together some mothers and daughters I knew, to have a conference that focused on building a strong bond between mother and daughter.

As I began to plan, the country began one of the worst pandemics it has seen in 100 years. The pandemic changed the way the world operated; therefore, I too, had to make an adjustment. With that adjustment, I decided to create a Facebook group called Mothers & Daughters, in which we could gather, support, encourage, and inspire each other on this journey. Knowing that my journey as a daughter and a mother was not all peaches and cream, I believed we could come together, ask questions pray for each other, and through our experiences, provide insight on how we pushed our way through some of the toughest moments in our lives.

As the Facebook group began to grow outside of my circle of friends and associates, I wanted to enhance our time together. Therefore, I was led to start Feature Friday. Feature Friday is when we feature one of our mother and daughter teams, and they get to share a part of their story.

As the mothers began to share, I found some of their stories to be absolutely amazing, and what was more intriguing, was several had prefaced their stories with, "I never told anyone this," or "I didn't know if I should share this, but I *hope it blesses someone." From this, the book you hold in your hands was birthed.*

I know we all have a story, yet those that are willing to tell it will be the ones that transform lives. There is a theory called "The Wounded Healer", first introduced by Carl Jung, and later developed by Marion Conti-O'Hare as "The Nurse as Wounded Healer", that addresses the effective, or ineffective, coping strategies after exposure to, or experiencing personal trauma. It explains that if trauma is dealt with effectively, the pain is consciously recognized, transformed, and transcended into healing. This process ultimately leads to healing, despite the remaining scars.

I believe we are all "Wounded Healers" in the respect of turning our pain into healing for ourselves and others. As you read through these stories of the brave women who chose to tell a part of their life's journey, may you find the courage to live, and the strength to rise above your circumstances, so that you may also become a "Wounded Healer".

~ *Jacqueline Pitt* ~

~ Dedication ~

Jackie: This book is dedicated to my mom, Wilma Levora Boston...you were always enough. And to my Aunt Dinah Satterthewaite, for standing in the gap.

Aboe: I dedicate this chapter to everyone that has triumphed great obstacles, despite having valid reasons to fail. I pray that you manifest greatness in the midst of adversity. Last, but definitely not least, I dedicate this chapter to the two women who have imparted wisdom, understanding, and unconditional love unto me...my mother Lorraine Anderson and Della Kwot.

Alicia: I want to dedicate this chapter to all the women who have intentionally poured into my life, due to the potential they saw. And to my children and grandchildren, who keep me humble, determined and focused.

Carolyn: This book is dedicated to my husband James, because without you, there would be no JOI!

Charlotte: Love has no boundaries. I dedicate this book, and my chapter, to my daughter, Sasha, and son, Raphael.

Onita: To my two daughters, Destiny and Janaye, thank you for giving me the courage to keep going and to keep growing. Your love has lifted me up, and helped me to walk when I felt I could no longer move. I love you both.

Yashica: I am dedicating this book to my daughter, NaCoria Donye. As you read, please note, there is not a perfect blueprint, just the blueprint we create. Love you always. Your mom.

~ About The Author ~

Jacqueline Pitt

Jacqueline Pitt was born and raised in Eastern North Carolina. She attended the University of North Carolina at Chapel Hill, and completed her degree in nursing at Columbus State University. She has been a nurse for over 24 years.

Jackie, as she prefers to be called, became a licensed minister in 2015. She has worked diligently in financial services as a financial coach since 2008. As an entrepreneur, she is the co-owner of Healing

Hands Nursing Services and a health coach. She is an online franchise owner.

She is also the founder of the Facebook group Mothers & Daughters, which inspired this book, and founder of both Reveal, Inc., and a ministry, Mind Changing Living (MCL).

Jackie and her husband of 34 years, Robert, have four beautiful daughters , Valonda, Akilah, Kanisha & Alisha; three from their union and one bonus daughter, a wonderful son-in-law, Peter, and three grandchildren, Elijah, Eliah, and Elise.

Though life did not go the way she planned, God allowed the desires of her heart to manifest in spite of. She has lived and traveled around the world and country. She now resides in South Carolina.

As one who desires to see others walk in their full potential in all areas of their life (spiritual, physical, and financial), Jackie encourages and promotes the development of the authentic self.

One of Jackie's favorite sayings is, "Life is about choices. Choose wisely."

Jackie desires for others to Flourish, or to suddenly perform or develop in an impressively successful way. Read along on Jackie's life journey and see how she overcame life's obstacles in order to Flourish.

FLOURISH

(an instance of suddenly performing or developing in an impressively successful way)

By

Jacqueline Pitt

"It's not where you start, but where you finish that counts." ~Zig Ziglar~

Being a three-year-old can be filled with many surprises. It is at that age that you assert your new-found freedom. You can do everything yourself. As a matter of fact, you can throw a massive temper tantrum if anyone tries to help you do something that you have firmly decided you can do yourself. Everything is "mine" and you have been established as the tyrant of the household. You see life as a game. You enjoy playing with your dolls, and everything is catered around appeasing you. Life is great, right? Not really. Not for this three-year-old.

Let me give you a little background of how it started. I was born into adversity. I know, you are probably thinking, *How many of us aren't?* Let me help you understand. My mom was 16 years old, and my dad was 19 years old when I was born. I'm sure as with many young teenage relationships, infatuation was the driving force. From what I was told my mom's measurements were 36-24-36, and if you know the song, you will finish with, *"What a winning hand."* My dad was tall, dark, handsome, and he had what the kids today call swag. They probably were head over heels for each other as young lovers tend to be.

Not too long after my mom got pregnant with me, my dad headed off to serve in the Vietnam War. He didn't stay long, but long enough to return home with PTSD, and a diagnosis of Paranoid Schizophrenia. Here is where life, as I knew it, begins.

There is a time for everything under the sun, but did you know there is a place for everyone in the Son? There is a time where we realize that which comes first is not always which leads. We all were created on

> *We all were created on purpose and for a purpose.*

purpose and for a purpose. However, there are moments in time where that purpose is birthed through adversity. Such adversity has a tendency to overshadow that which was destined from the creation of the world. It has been said that on the other side of struggle is purpose, but many never seem to realize their purpose, because all they focus on is the mess before them.

Have you ever been looking for something, searched diligently to find it, and after taking a moment from the search, you inevitably return to the very mess you left behind, only to find it in the very first spot you searched? That's how life is. We search our whole lives in the same place, only to take a moment away, and return to find everything we were looking for once our eyes are no longer distracted by the mess. Our heart was open, but our eyes were blinded to what was right in front of us.

1966 was like any other year that had come and gone, but September 16 of that year would change the course of history for me. That was the year I became a daughter. I was born to a sweet-sixteen, pecan brown, beautifully shaped (as I was told), girl from North Carolina. I'm not sure if she knew the significance of my birth at that age, but I believe somewhere deep down in the pit of her soul, she knew her life had changed.

Long before "it" happens, we have an inclination that there has been a shift. A shift not just in the earth, but in the atmosphere. Something within our soul validates the change, but because of our spiritual disconnect, we dismiss it as just a funny feeling, or "something told me". To ignore this spiritual inclination, the red flag warning us that we are out of alignment with the order of God, proves detrimental to our life's journey. I am convinced by what I know now, that had my mom

realized my birth would change the course of our

lives, and leave a lasting impact for years to come, I

may not have been born. But I was.

My earliest recollection of my mother and

father was when I was three years old. I remember

riding in a light green car, sitting in the backseat

enroute from somewhere. All seemed to be

pleasant until my mom said she had to use the

bathroom. I can remember the music playing, yet a

stillness was in the air. My dad pulled over to a

service station to get gas, and my mom reached for

the door handle.

My dad asked, "Where do you think you are

going?"

My mom said, "I have to use the bathroom."

My dad refused to let her get out of the car. She resisted until he hit her in the face. She stopped resisting, but he didn't stop hitting. I saw the blood running down her face, as I sat in the back seat screaming, crying, and pleading for my dad to stop.

I'm not sure when, but he eventually stopped. She did not need to use the bathroom anymore because she had more pressing concerns. What is interesting, I do not remember my brother being there, but of course he must have been, for he was only one. As a matter of fact, I do not remember anything else about that day after that moment.

There are moments in our lives that we will never forget, moments that are etched in our memories forever. Moments that we wish we could change, or at least have the opportunity to replace, but unfortunately, life does not allow do-overs, at least for things you have no control over.

What only took moments to create, unknowingly created many years of pain and shame. It was because of this pain and shame, I had to spend many of my days raising my mom when she should have been raising me. The depths of the abuse can be compared to a stubborn weed in a beautifully displayed garden. As you know, a weed can sometimes grow unnoticed in the garden, and before you realize it, the weeds have taken over, and choked the life out of your garden.

My mom was soft-spoken, loved to laugh, and was one of the most giving people you would ever meet. One thing I know for sure, her generosity was a characteristic and biblical principle that had been passed down through the generations. What others may not see as valuable, God uses for His glory. I remember the gentleness in her voice and the kindness in her eyes, despite the trials of her journey.

No matter what life has to offer, we are always receiving or giving something in exchange. Think about that for a moment. I challenge you to make a list, good or bad, of those things you have received, or given, during the course of your life.

If we took inventory or assessed our lives periodically, we may discover we have spent too much time being consumed by people and things that were not designed for us to live the abundant life God promised. How often do you take inventory?

Perhaps if my mother knew that the abundant life was inherently hers, she would have routinely taken an inventory of what she was collecting, and made the necessary adjustments to eliminate that which did not belong, and embrace that which remained. As kind and giving as my mother was, she never allowed herself to experience that which she gave to others.

One of my first lessons that my mother attempted to teach me, was to give to yourself that which you give to others. If this was a deliberate and intentional lesson, I would have taken heed and repeated what I saw.

Statistics show we remember 20% of what we hear, and 30% of what we see, and 80% of what we experience, so the impact of hearing, seeing, and experiencing is a far greater percentage.

My mom, in her confusion of who she was, was unable to create an environment for us that allowed my brother and I to thrive in our authentic selves. It wasn't that she did not desire to, it was because she did not know how to. Instead, I was taught to live in fear, tolerate the intolerable, and stay silent, even if I was screaming on the inside.

I later learned that one of my first memories shaped my future decisions. At the age of 6, I had experienced what psychologists would describe as adverse childhood experiences (ACEs). On the point scale for ACEs, I had 9 out of 10.

When you experience a thing often enough, it becomes your norm. The problem with this is, your normal is not "the normal." When you live in your normal long enough without a reality check, you believe everyone else is also living in the same place. You have no idea that the things you see, and the pain you are experiencing, does not belong to you. It has been placed in you by those who never knew you were an unwilling participant. I spent a large part of my younger years in the midst of abuse and uncertainty.

According to the CDC, ACEs are potentially traumatic events that occur in childhood (0-17 years), such as:

- *experiencing violence, abuse, or neglect*
- *witnessing violence in the home or community*
- *having a family member attempt or die by suicide*

Also included are aspects of the child's environment that can undermine their sense of safety, stability, and bonding such as growing up in a household with:

- *substance misuse*
- *mental health problems*
- *instability due to parental separation or household members being in jail or prison*

ACEs are linked to chronic health problems, mental illness, and substance misuse in adulthood. ACEs can also negatively impact education and job opportunities. However, ACEs can be prevented. How do we prevent it? By creating and sustaining safe, stable, nurturing relationships and environments for all children and families can prevent ACEs and help all children reach their full health and life potential.

In essence, we must do our part, not just as individuals, but as a society that does not judge, but supports those in need, whether it be domestic violence, substance abuse, or mental illness. When we see ourselves as the village, we refuse to allow

our village to be sabotaged by such things. As a

people, we understand the village is only as good

as the citizens. The stigma that comes along with

abuse or mental illness prevents individuals from

asking for help.

This is where my mom got stuck. She knew

she needed help, but was too ashamed to seek

help, because she did not want people talking

about her. My mom was later diagnosed with

bipolar disorder and manic depression. After years

of abuse, which literally took everything she had,

her self-esteem, her fight, her joy, her peace, and

her hope, she no longer flourished, but quietly

drifted away into a place that only she understood,

and left us on the outside looking in.

There were glimmers of hope with an occasional laugh here or there, but it was not lasting. I often asked myself what I could do to help her get out of that place. That place had to be lonely, and obviously sad by the look in her eyes. In her depressive state, she would not do much of anything. She would just suck her thumb as a source of comfort, and watch as we went on about our day. We would attempt to entertain her with hopes of helping her snap out it, but to no avail. I know now, no matter what we did, it would not have brought her back until she had finished searching in her head for a way out.

When I was around eight or so, my grandmother gave me the responsibility of looking after my mom and brother. She gave me specific instructions about what to do, and how to do it. I was told to make sure my mother and brother ate. If my mother attempted to go anywhere, I was to first try to stop her and if she did not listen, I was to come and get my grandmother.

Think about this for a moment...you are eight, and asked to care for your mother, and your brother, who is six. Imagine that weight on an eight-year-old. What's interesting is I never knew it was out of the ordinary for an eight-year-old to care for her mother.

When you live in your normal long enough without a reality check, you believe everyone else is living in the same place. What areas of your life have you spent doing the same thing so long that you have made it your norm?

To move from this space, you must first recognize you don't belong. Secondly, you must ask yourself do you want to be healed? I know you're thinking, but you were only eight. You are right, but regardless of your age, you must have the desire for change, or it will never happen. An infant learning to walk must have the desire to walk, or else they will never walk. That's why the infant falls down, and gets up again. Desire is the driving force, not their age. You must move expeditiously, or you may be soothed by the sways of comfort, and settle in the all so familiar place of your norm.

When I was ten, there was a shift in my norm. I remember the fifth grade as if it were yesterday. This was one of my best times during my school years, not only because my best friend was in my class, but also because this was the first time that I realized that I had a voice, and the power to say no. I was not a victim of my circumstances any longer.

Many days, I remember coming home from school, and my mom was sitting quietly on the porch, or in the living room sucking her thumb. Sometimes she was watching television; other times she would just sit there, seemingly lost in her own world.

When I asked, "How was your day," I would sometimes have to repeat myself more than once before she would snap out of the place in her mind to respond. These spells didn't last long. They would last only a moment, and then she would go right back to that place in her mind. When she retreated to that place, I often felt alone and sad.

As I walked home from school, I would imagine what was happening, or what conversations were being had, in the houses I passed. Was it like my house, with not much communication from the mom? Was the dad or stepdad present? Was mom making dinner for the family, or did she have snacks prepared when the children came home from school? Did she help them with their homework, or help them prepare for bed? I would make up these conversations as I went.

I believe so much of our survival depends on our ability to have conversations with ourselves about what we desire. Conversations about what God desires for us, versus what we desire. I, of course, at ten, did not realize the things I was speaking into the atmosphere would one day align with the desires of my heart. Those things we do not have can be manifested by what we speak. Speak those things that do not exist into existence.

How divine it is to walk in the ways of the Kingdom unaware. God is always watching over us, even when we are clueless of His presence. Through experience, I have learned that conversing with oneself is necessary. More importantly, it matters what we tell ourselves.

As with any words, they can build you up or tear you down. Today, I need you to speak life to yourself first, and even if you can't see it or believe it, you are building a powerful fortress that will not be easily broken. The things I told myself at ten, such as, "It will be different when I grow up," or "Things will not always be like this," or "You are ok," all provided a mental barrier during one of the toughest times in my life, when I was 14.

> *Those things we do not have can be manifested by what we speak.*

I thought ten was tough, but I had no idea 14 was coming! My interest shifted, I started my menstrual cycle, and oh, how that brought about a change. I didn't see myself as attractive. I was teased about my complexion, and desired to be like everyone else. I had no idea that most girls at this age were battling the same, or similar insecurities as me. One thing I believed for sure, was that those girls had someone to talk to about all the things that were wrong in their lives.

Unfortunately, I became distant, and full of myself, at this point. I was embarrassed by my mom's psychological disorder, and angry about my parents not being together. They had divorced when I was in elementary school. All of these things happening at the same time, caused my life to be a mess. Not just a mess, but a hot mess. If you grew up in a black household, you knew this meant trouble! This is also about the time I met my first unofficial (because I was not allowed to date) boyfriend, who was 18, four years older than me. As you can imagine, this added fuel to an already complicated situation.

I was confused. I really did not know how to handle any of this. I wished I had someone to talk to. Not just anyone, but my mom. I became more pressured to fit in. I was looking for normal in all the wrong places.

When your perspective is distorted, your outcome is also distorted. I did not have a role model. I felt as if I were alone. If a decision had to be made, I was the one that needed to make it. I knew my mom was my mom, but I also knew she could not make decisions on my behalf. She couldn't help me; she couldn't even help herself.

I just found out recently from our oldest daughter that my golden birthday was 16. Your golden birthday happens during the year in which you turn the same age as your birthdate. The year I turned 16 was far from golden. My life changed forever during that year.

I was still trying to fit in with the crowd, and at the same time, trying to discover who I was, and what I wanted in life. I knew what I didn't want. I did not want to be stuck in small-town U.S.A. for the rest of my life. I wanted to go to college, live in the city, and travel the world. Even though I had no plans on how this would happen, I knew it would.

I had to make a decision, but I didn't have anyone to talk to. I went to the health department to get birth control. I knew this was what I should do, but I was afraid of what people would think? Would someone tell my mom? What would she say if she found out? Would this make her angry? Would she go into a state of depression? Isn't it amazing how fear and what others think, can talk us out of making a decision? What decisions have you allowed to be gripped by fear?

Fear can disrupt our entire thought process and make us do things we would not normally do. Fear does not belong to us! It was not given to us;

therefore, it was acquired through experiences. What we were given was power, love and a sound mind (2 Timothy 1:7). We ALL are equipped when we enter into this world, however, our circumstances, what we see, and what we hear, transform our belief system into one of doubt and insecurities. I decided to stay and get the birth control.

Wait.. I'm what?

This cannot be happening! How did I make the right decision at the wrong time? I was pregnant. I had no idea how I would tell my mom. This would be a painful reminder of all the things that kept her bound for so long.

I was so disappointed in myself. I had BIG plans. I would go to college at UNC at Chapel Hill. Once I finished college, I would travel the world, maybe stay in another country for a while. One day, I would get married and have children, but that one day came without warning, and I was not married. I was ashamed.

My mom and I both eventually got over it. I knew what I had to do for my little girl. I had to continue with my plans, even if it meant I had to sacrifice. My mom was doing a lot better, maybe because she was taking her medication now. I got accepted into UNC at Chapel Hill. My mom agreed to watch my baby girl while I went to college.

She said, "I don't want your life to turn out like mine. I don't want you to get stuck." So off to college I went.

Life was seemingly going as planned, even after a few bumps in the road. My mom got her GED. I had the opportunity to be the first one from my maternal side of the family to go to college. For the first time, I had a chance to not be concerned about taking care of anyone except me. I'm not sure if that was a good thing or not.

Freedom without a plan, is like winning the lottery after you have been poor all your life. You do not know how to handle it, so you waste it. I finished my first year of college with 1.9 G.P.A. I was missing home, and even more so, my sweet girl. I continued on for one more year, and then I gave in to my emotions and left college. The place I dreaded the most, I was returning to.

After being home for a while, I realized I could not stay there. I had to get out. How? I was not sure. I just knew I could not stay. I cannot recall how long I was there before my first boyfriend asked me to marry him. I joined him at his first duty station out of basic training, Fort Riley, Kansas. There we began our first chance at marriage. By the time we left Fort Riley, we had baby girl number two.

As we settled down at our new duty station in Columbus, Georgia, I was ready for a change. I was grateful for the opportunity to start traveling, even though it was not the way I originally intended. It's amazing how God will give you what you want, even if you do not recognize He did. I was not traveling the world yet, but I was a long way from home.

A dream deferred is not a dream denied. Maybe you have dreamed of doing something. If it hasn't come to fruition, don't close the door and throw away the key. Keep the faith and trust that God had a plan from the beginning.

In the fall of 1993, I started college again, this time with a new perspective. I had a family. I was in a different place emotionally and mentally, and I knew what I was there for. I had never worked so hard at, or for something. What a difference clarity makes.

A perfect plan may not look like what you intended; it may have some bumps in the road and few detours along the way, but when you allow your perspective to shift, your journey will become easier to bear.

> *I know that you don't have to fit in, because you were truly born to stand out.*

As a mother, who was once a daughter, I know the challenges of living in both worlds. I know through ACEs that domestic violence runs deeper than physical scares. I know it has roots that run through the depths of generations with many different manifestations. I know the pain of being a child, yet having the responsibilities of an adult.

I now know that mental illness is nothing to be ashamed of, yet the scars it leaves behind can take a lifetime to heal. I know we must tell those that suffer with a psychological disorder that it is okay to seek help. I know that no matter what statistics say, God has the final say so. I know that you don't have to fit in, because you were truly born to stand out. I know that many are the plans in a man's heart, but it is the Lord's purpose that prevails (Proverbs 19:21). I know now that I was never alone, but had been protected, guided, and loved from the beginning.

I was purposed to flourish in adversity, so that my story could one day be the balm that heals many.

Connect with Jacqueline

Instagram: @Mindchangingliving

Email: MothersDaughtersRwe@gmail.com

Twitter: @JacqueAPitt

~ About The Author ~

Aboe Banks

Aboe Banks was born and raised in the small town of Plymouth, North Carolina, until the age eight. She was born to a southern county girl and a Sudan-African native. Her very existence was already a very interesting one given her diverse cultural background.

Life itself doesn't come with instructions. So, what happens when you're thrown a curve ball, and no one has even taught you how to play catch?

At a very young age, Aboe became what society would call a statistic. Life hasn't always given her lemonade, however, she quickly learned how to sweeten the lemons.

Aboe's story is one that is too often seen but never really told. Although she has suffered through childhood traumas, such as molestation, parental substance addiction, and teenage pregnancy, she has not allowed that to be her defining attribute.

It's not uncommon to experience obstacles in life. It is her hope that the transparency of her struggles brings clarity to those in need that read her story.

Today, Aboe continues to be a work in progress, breaking barriers within, and motivating her daughters, through open dialogue, and creating a space conducive to healthy expression.

Travel along through Aboe's life, and see how she uses Vinegar to position herself into purpose.

PURPOSED POSITIONING TAKES

V-ision

I-ntention

N-avigation

E-agerness

G-ratitude

A-cceptance

R-eclamation

By

Aboe Banks

What do you do, when you don't know what to do? Do you do anything at all? Or, do you pretend until you eventually come clear about what to do? As for me, it has always been the latter.

This picture of a tall, voluptuous, slightly mysterious person the world sees today is all but perfect. In fact, the person I present to the world on any given day is as strong as an ox, with courage that can challenge the mightiest of lions. However, what lies beneath the surface is a story that too often is seen but never told.

I would always ask myself; what would you say if you had the chance to be completely transparent? I know that true healing comes from digging deep into the grungy stuff that leaves imprints within our core. Ultimately, this is what shapes how we are seen by the world.

In the Spring of 1980, the world was introduced to a little girl named Aboe Nyijwon Kwot, weighing in at eight pounds, four ounces. I was born to a southern country girl and a Sudanese-African man in the city of Raleigh, North Carolina. My parents met in college during a psychology class at North Carolina Central University (NCCU). The entanglement of two very different worlds had its own set of challenges which led to a very brief marriage.

After my parents' separation, I became the product of a single-mother household. My mother moved us into the projects of our hometown of

Plymouth, North Carolina, and this would be the

place I called home until the age of eight. My father

visited often, so although he wasn't present in the

home, I still had the comfort of knowing that he

was always nearby. Life with my mom was

ordinary, and by ordinary, I mean full of hugs and

kisses and nurturing. If we lacked, I never knew. I

was an only child, so I never had to fight for

attention or affection, until one day I realized that

something wasn't the same.

Somewhere between the ages of seven and

eight, my mother lost her way. What I had come to

know as loving and nurturing, changed into feelings

of abandonment, fear, shame, and guilt. My

mother had become addicted to crack cocaine. I

can remember some days I would walk to the homes of nearby relatives and family friends, to sit with them until my mom returned. I learned quickly that whatever my mother was doing, it had to have been something noteworthy.

Growing up in a small town has it peaks, and by the same token, it also has its valleys. News often spreads like a wildfire, good, bad, or indifferent. Unfortunately for me, my mother was now the latest talk of the dirty gossip that traveled throughout the town. As a child, I was rendered helpless. I wanted so much for all the things I'd heard about my mother to be untrue. But as time went on, it became very clear to me that life as I once knew it was about to change forever.

I believe wholeheartedly that in her very best efforts my mother attempted to shield me from any hurt, harm, or foul. But, how do you protect your child against the wolf dressed in sheep's clothing? One of the people she entrusted to care for me during her self-sabotaging sabbaticals was the very person that snatched my innocence. It first started as touching. Up until then, the basic human need for touch was still normal to me. Then the slight touching became increasingly uncomfortable. Later, in life I would come to learn that I was being groomed. This happened a few times before I was forced to perform oral sex on this person.

I didn't have a clue as to what was being asked of me, but I knew that it was wrong, and it

made my tiny body ripple with gut-wrenching fear.
Like many victims, the thought of shedding light
upon this violation caused me much emotional
turmoil. Still, somehow, I managed to dismiss my
own feelings because I knew that my mother was
sick, and I couldn't add to her dismay. In fact, I
wanted to do for her the very thing she failed to do
for me...protect her. This is when I learned how to
devalue and minimize myself, and excuse bad
behavior.

As time went on, my mother became even
more dependent on self-medicating. Eventually,
she reached out to my father asking for help. She
made the decision that the drug would supersede
her ability to continue to be responsible for me.

Not long after witnessing my mother have a nervous breakdown, I found myself now living with my father and stepmother. I really didn't know if this arrangement would be better, but it did offer me a sense of security, even if came with stipulations. Although, I no longer had to fear being taking advantage of by people I was told to trust, the feelings of abandonment and fear remembered my name, and found my new address. But what happened next would open a floodgate of traumas no one could have prepared me for.

I learned about God at an early age. My grandmother had given me this little prayer devotional book. Whenever it would rain, I would open the book and start reading. I gauged how well God was listening to me by how many times I heard thunder. I told myself that God could only really hear me during the thunderstorms. Unbeknownst to me at the time, this coping mechanism I'd developed would be my saving grace.

At the tender age of 14, I found myself pregnant. To say that I was afraid was an understatement. I was completely terrified. I now had another secret to bear that was killing me slowly. The voice that I could have had was taken long ago. I had learned to function in total chaos. I told myself that my very existence was such a strain that even my mother had to create an escape route. My father was the unlucky person left, that was as equally responsible for me, so he had no other choice but to raise me.

Not only was I pregnant, but the father of my child was my stepbrother. I made the decision then that I would keep quiet and pray that something different would happen, and it did.

At 42 weeks gestation, I gave birth to my first daughter. I didn't have to be told that my daughter's life was nothing short of a miracle. I knew it was. The fear that captured me at the age of seven, was the same fear that kept me from seeking help and medical care the entire nine months of pregnancy. The first time I saw a doctor was the night I gave birth to my beautiful baby. Sure, I prayed that God would make all of it go away. I just couldn't understand how He would allow this to happen. Did He not know that I am the same little girl that would pray to Him during the storms? Being young and naïve gave way to many failures. I experienced life as a tragedy and now here I was, the mother to a baby, while still a baby myself.

I moved back home with my mother in December of 1994, two months after giving birth to my first child. It was a long time coming. By now, my mother had done a complete 180. Her life was much different than I remembered when she left me at the age of eight. After six long years, we were back together but our dynamic was forever changed. Yes, I was happy to be back with my mother, but I was afraid that it would be short-lived.

My expectations of life itself in that moment were very grim and perplexing. I still couldn't figure out why God would entrust me with the task of motherhood at such an early age. The answer to that question would still be a long time coming.

As the years went by, I navigated through life with all the baggage that had been dumped in my lap since I was a little girl. In 1998, I gave birth to my second daughter, and graduated from high school. Now, here I am a mother of two, still carrying around trauma, still acting like I am ok, knowing that deep down in the fabric of my being, the ground beneath me was about to cave.

In the summer of 1999, I decided that small-town living was not for me. The only thing I had was a high school education. Unfortunately, living in a small town made decent jobs hard to come by, especially the ones that offered any real compensation.

So, once again, I found myself moving back to South Carolina with my father. Shortly after settling back down, I met my last two daughters' father. That relationship was long, hard, and full of lessons that would foster the beginning of my path to healing, but not before hitting plenty more bumps in the road.

I never would have imagined that I would be fingerprinted or have to take a mugshot. But as life would have it, one time wasn't good enough, so I blew caution to the wind and repeated it again. What my close family called "anger issues", I now know was my response to unhealed trauma. Often, I would project my anger, due to my lack of self-control. My children endured so much due to my inability to address my pain.

As if my childhood wasn't tumultuous enough, I further complicated things. My lack of self-love landed me in an abusive relationship that almost took my life. I allowed my children to be exposed to drugs being sold out of our home, and physical abuse. It's funny, life has a way of bringing everything back to your remembrance.

When I looked in the mirror, all I could see was darkness and terror. I knew that I wanted differently for myself and my children, but up until this point, I did not know how to obtain it. Somehow, I tricked myself into believing that I was different, that I wasn't the mother that I had been born unto. Truthfully, I was the exact replica of the mother that I had been given.

I lost everything, including my place to live. My child was even compromised because of my shortcomings. I always thought of "rock bottom" as a place of pure intentional hell. No one ever told me that "rock bottom" was a place for purposed retribution.

I can recall crying out to God that I was ready. Honestly, I really didn't know what I was ready for, but what I was sure about is that I was tired, and something had to change. I knew I had to release the baggage that I carried. Some of the baggage was my own, but most wasn't even mine to hold. I was broken, I was tired, and I was still a mother to four innocent people that deserved better than what I had given them.

I started listening to self-help audios and watching one of my favorite television shows, *Iyanla Fix My Life*. I realized that I had not taken responsibility for myself. I learned that taking responsibility was still taking care of "me", regardless of who or what caused the trauma. Accountability was holding myself accountable for all the self-inflicted wounds I caused. My response to pain was so far removed from reality, I was crippled and didn't even know it. I felt more comfortable being an option than living my life as a priority, and this was the same message I was passing along to my children.

If I must be completely transparent, I'm still learning. Every day, I find new layers of old outdated idioms that no longer serve me or my purpose. I used to look at my life and think to myself this is what it looks like to be unlovable. There is no way God would allow terrible things to happen to people that were worthy of being loved.

As I became more involved in my spiritual journey, my understanding of the Creator also changed. I started to see that God truly doesn't put more on us than we can bear. One day, I remembered what I had been told by a lady I met in church. She said to me, "WOW, I see you," and then she left me with two scriptures that keep me grounded to this day.

- Matthew 22:14: *"For many are called, but few are chosen,"* and

- Luke 12:48 *"...For to everyone to whom much is given, from him much will be required..."*

Presently, I'm still a work in progress. I've only just begun this total transformation. I have no accolades to report, or degrees that I have obtained. However, what I do have is a rebirth of identity that reflects God's light and love.

I know now that I am not my past, and I am not my mother's past. My cross is mine to bear, and with clarity, I speak unto my daughters that their lives will be sustained, and always be guided by the Creator.

Connect with Aboe

Email: aboebanks@gmail.com

About The Author

Alicia P. Harris MA, LPC, LAC, NCC

Alicia Patricia Harris is a native of Paterson, New Jersey, where she graduated from the infamous Eastside High School under the leadership of the late Joe Clark.

Currently, Alicia is a Licensed Professional Counselor, Licensed Addictions Counselor, and the Owner/Therapist at Brella Counseling Services LLC, where her mission is to assist individuals in the pursuit of positive mental health and wellness. She loves working in her community for causes such as domestic violence, homelessness, youth leadership, and public speaking.

Alicia has been featured in articles written by The MinorityEye and Carolina Panorama digital newspapers for her service to the community, and hosted the first annual Alopecia Awareness Event in 2018.

She has been interviewed on OnPoint! with Cynthia Hardy for her contribution to the sexual assault and domestic violence documentary, "HUSH No More" in 2018.

Alicia is currently pursuing a Ph.D. in Counseling Education and Supervision at the University of the Cumberlands in Williamsburg, Kentucky. She was chosen as a fellow of the St. Louis Business Diversity & Inclusion Program for the 2020-2021 year. This fellowship assists participants in enhancing professional areas such as networking, leadership and civic engagement.

Alicia's favorite quote is, "People don't care how much you know until they know how much you care." Travel on this journey with Alicia as she is empowered to take off her mask and live in her truth.

UNMASKING TO EMPOWER

By

Alicia P. Harris

This is my story, and I will tell it if I want to. That is what I say to myself every time I am asked to share my story with an audience, or an individual, that could benefit from hearing a piece of my history.

See, we all have a story. Some of us are more comfortable sharing than others, but deep inside, we have all had some traumatic, as well as amazing experiences. I am of the belief that our stories are ours to tell initially, then if others choose to reference, share, or repeat them, at least we had the opportunity to deliver them from our lived experience.

So, take a literary journey with me as I share a moment in time from my life. I pray that my story will bring about encouragement, courage, and perseverance to those who read it. I am choosing to be vulnerable in sharing with you the mask I once wore, and the work I did, not only to remove it, but to destroy it permanently.

Women oftentimes wear many masks to conceal the turmoil going on inside. They carry scars and hurt around like a bag of bricks, and are unsure of how to unload them so they can run toward freedom. Part of the problem, is that most women are too "masked up" to provide healthy direction or advice to their sisters along the way. On the other hand, there are those who could shed light on the road to freedom, but won't, as they cannot see the value in sharing their story.

My name is Alicia P. Harris, the P is for Patricia, which by the way is the same middle name that my mom had. My birthday is on what I consider to be a national holiday, and that is March 31st. I was born in Brooklyn, New York, and lived in East New York prior to moving to New Jersey. Once in New Jersey, my family and I lived in the city of Camden.

For anyone who has ever heard anything about Camden, it was, and is, a rough place to live, but my family always made my home a haven. It was as if I lived on my own little oasis. Family and friends were there, and I even had a dog. Those were some of the happiest times of my childhood. Well, at least for a while anyway.

By the time I turned four, my parents had split, and I was the pawn in a nasty custody battle. I remember a lot of whispering amongst the grownups in my life, and extreme tension. You see,

my mom refused to allow me to stay in the

environment that nurtured me. The environment

in which I was most familiar, and the same

environment that I credit for my fondest

memories. The reason for her refusal was that she

had relocated to another city and demanded that I

live with her.

Well, my mother was granted her wish, and

I was uprooted from my familiar environment and

deposited into the city of Paterson. It was here

where my young eyes were opened to things I

never knew existed. It was this city that taught me

that life was tough, and to make it you had to be

even tougher. I went from playing in a fenced in

yard in Camden, with a dog, and seeing my

grandparents, aunts, and dad daily, to becoming a

latch-key kid in a concrete jungle once known as

the Grand Street Projects.

Life was full of challenges for me and my

newly single mother. You see, my mom was not

wise with her money, nor did she create and stick

to a budget. As a result, my life was genuinely like a

box of chocolates...I

never knew what to

At an early age, I realized that my voice did not carry much weight.

expect. There were

moments in which I

became more

concerned about my basic needs versus what

cartoon I would watch next. There were instances

in which next meal options were scarce and living

arrangements were in jeopardy. All because of my mom's lack of financial intelligence.

At an early age, I realized that my voice did not carry much weight. I was told what to do, when to do it, and how it would be done, and if those directives were not followed, well, it did not make for a good outcome. My mom was strict and no-nonsense. Now, she was loving and supportive, but she had a lot on her plate as a single parent, so certain things were just not tolerated.

She was a strong black woman, and attempted to instill that in me. However, being the new kid to the projects who knew nothing about street smarts, I became an easy target for bullies. This became a sport for them and there were almost daily instances with one girl. Coming from my haven surrounded by family, I never had to worry about violence or defending myself, so going up against these bullies was not something I was confident in or successful at.

That is where mom's strength came in. She taught me how to defend myself not only physically, but verbally. The ability to be assertive was not an issue for her, and she did not mind putting people in their place. She used to say, "You teach people how to treat you, so be a good teacher. Say what you mean and mean what you say!"

My mom was a force to be reckoned with, and I viewed her as impenetrable. Despite growing up around all that strength, there were years that went by in which I just wanted to have the love, acceptance, and approval of my dad.

Growing up without him in the home was difficult. When I did visit him, I still felt alone and like a burden. We were not close at all, and looking back, I am not sure that my dad knew how to be, which began to shape my viewpoint on relationships.

I became an over-achiever, thinking that performance would gain his attention, approval, and most of all, his love. To my disappointment, my efforts were fruitless, and no matter how many Honor Roll certificates I received, or trophies I won, my dad and I were not connected emotionally. That was more detrimental than I realized at the time. My experience with boys, and ultimately men, was unhealthy. After all, I had a faulty blueprint.

The relationship with my dad was so strained, that I looked to other men to fill the void his absence left in me. I spent most of my time trying to please them by performing. If I needed to change my hair, I did that. If I needed to be less outgoing, I did that. And when it came to tolerating negative behaviors, I did that. I could truly attest to the statement found on t-shirts that says, *"Been there, done that, and got the t-shirt."*

After a series of bad relationships, at 16, I became pregnant with my oldest daughter. By 18, I was married, and by 20, my son was born. It was during this marriage that I experienced domestic violence, and that violence changed my life forever.

It was the best of times and it was the worst of times. That is how I would sum up the three-and-a-half years of my life that I spent being married to my first husband. When it was good, it was memorable, but when it was bad, it was horrific! So much so, I almost died at the hands of a man that was broken, controlling, and insecure, although it did not start off that way.

I met who I thought was my knight in shining armor. He was older than I was, and had a car, which back then was the coolest thing. I quickly became enamored with him, and thought I was the luckiest girl in the world. He was tall, dark, and handsome, and he listened to my every word. For the first time in my young life, someone was listening to me, and seemed to be interested in how I viewed the world.

In the beginning things were magical. There were flowers, jewelry, and public displays of affection. At 17, I had no idea of what my love language was, but he surely was speaking what I wanted, better yet, what I needed to hear. The butterflies talked about in the love stories you see on tv were certainly real for me, and they lasted for months. The sound of his voice made my whole body quiver, and to hold his hand or kiss his lips caused me to mentally visualize myself in paradise. As far as I was concerned, we could be the only two people left on earth and that was ok.

To my astonishment, this fairy tale quickly turned into a suspense thriller. It began subtle at first, with comments like, "Why are you wearing your hair like that?" or "Why do you need to hang out with your friends so much?" Or the best one of all, "I just get so jealous, because I want to spend as much time with you as I can. I miss you so much when I am not with you."

Now, to a 17-year-old girl, those things may sound trivial and

> *He wanted me isolated and void of close friendships, and inserted himself into every area of my life like a computer virus.*

flattering at the same time. However, this was the typical motive of control by my abuser. He wanted to dictate how I wore my hair, to include the length. He wanted me isolated and void of close friendships, and inserted himself into every area of my life like a computer virus. All this so that he

could eventually execute his ultimate plan.

Unfortunately, I was too naïve and broken to see it.

Broken in the sense that I

> *For an abuser, a woman with low self-esteem and self-worth is an easy target.*

was a young girl who did

not have a healthy

relationship with her dad,

whose self-esteem was

poor, and who felt that any male attention was a

sign of acceptance and love.

Poor self-esteem and self-worth have a way

of distorting your view, not only of yourself, but

also of your place in society and the world. These

two culprits will lead you to believe that you have

nothing of value to contribute, and can cause you

to be silent in instances where you need to be screaming from the rooftops.

This is where I was at 17. My voice had been taken at an early age, and I grew up allowing others to orchestrate my words as if they were the ventriloquist, and I, the puppet.

For an abuser, a woman with low self-esteem and self-worth is an easy target. They know how to lay on the charm and flattery, and then once you are under their spell, they morph into the next character and begin with control tactics.

I share with women often that an abuser is like a thief versus a robber.

I share with women often that an abuser is like a thief versus a robber. A thief takes little by little, until you look up one day, and realize that all has been lost, that you have been taken further than you planned to go, and sacrificed far more than you intended. On the other hand, a robber sticks the gun or knife in your face, and takes whatever they want without playing nice first. After all, who would go on a second date with a person who slapped you across the face on the first date?

Speaking of slapping across the face, I remember a time when my husband and I went to the local auto parts store in Paterson to purchase some parts for his car. While in the store, I ran into an old classmate, who was a male, and we spoke to each other. I immediately introduced my husband to him, and the three of us stood making small talk for about seven minutes before we left. I got into the car and buckled my seat belt. When I turned to face my husband, I was met with a back-hand slap across the face, and was told that I had not been given permission to speak to another man. The throbbing in my cheek and the hot tears on my face will never be forgotten.

This was one of many incidents of physical abuse I endured throughout my marriage, and they were always followed by flowers and other material things, to include limousine rides and dinners at fancy restaurants. Each time, a heartfelt apology was coupled with tears and promises to never do it again. That would last for a short period of time, until I did something else to set him off, and was met with either a chokehold or a fist to the face.

Most of the time, I endured the beatings and mental anguish silently. However, there was one time that I attempted to get help by going to my doctor. On this occasion, he had choked me so bad that the blood vessels in both my eyes burst, leaving the whites of my eyes bright red. He allowed me to go to the doctor, because he was afraid that someone would say something, since my bruises could not be hidden.

At the appointment, the doctor asked what happened, and I lied, stating that it was a reaction to some outdated Visine. My heart and soul were screaming out, "*I WAS ABUSED*!" But I would not allow the words to come out of my mouth. It was at that moment that I hoped the doctor would probe with additional questions, that he would articulate the question to make it easy for me to just say, "*YES!*" To my disappointment, that did not happen, and instead a prescription for eye drops was written, and I was sent on my way, back to my abuser.

Medical students are being trained in most states on intimate partner violence, and the signs to look for when a woman presents for medical services. I have had the opportunity to participate in these sessions with a local university by sharing my story, and allowing students to ask probing questions, and gain real-time understanding through the lens of a survivor.

Abused women are great at wearing "masks". They know the excuses to use that coincide with their bruises. I cannot tell you how many times I used the story about falling down the stairs, or bumping into a wall because I was walking through the house in the dark. It is imperative that doctors, nurses, etc., are astute in noticing the signs of an abused woman. They need to ask questions in such a manner that gives the

> *The most dangerous time for an abused woman is when she attempts to leave.*

woman an easy way to admit to experiencing violence in the home. Then, be ready to provide resources if the woman is ready to receive them.

The most dangerous time for an abused woman is when she attempts to leave. Statistics show that a victim attempts to leave at least seven times before finally leaving for good, and that a woman has a 70% chance of being murdered within two weeks of leaving an abusive relationship. Timing and sensitivity is vital.

Unfortunately, the previously described incidents of violence were not the last for me. He just became more careful in where he placed the bruises so there would be no more doctor visits. This went on for another year before I found the courage to speak up about the abuse. Courage was needed for several reasons. I needed courage to tell my mother that I was being abused. Remember my mother, the strong black woman I spoke of earlier? I had heard her say on several occasions that she thought a woman was stupid to allow a man to put his hands on her, not realizing that her own daughter was suffering through this same situation.

In the three-and-a-half years of my marriage and abuse, I never told my mother, or anyone for that matter. I kept hearing her words play over and over in my head, and for fear of being perceived as stupid, silence strangled my voice.

Courage was needed to stand up to the monster, who at our wedding, vowed to love and cherish me until death did us part.

Lastly, courage was needed to make the choice to leave a destructive environment with two small children, not knowing how I would make it on my own. What I did know, was that this situation was exacerbating, and mentally, I was at the end of my rope. If I did not do something soon, my husband would take my life, or I would succumb to the thoughts of taking my own life as a means of escape.

Thoughts of suicide were not uncommon during that time in my life. I rationalized it as a means of being in control of what happens to me, as well as to avoid being hurt ever again. Even as I write these words over 30 years later, I cringe at the fact that suicide was considered as one of my escape plans. During that time, I was a desperate, hopeless, shell of a woman, who felt like she had no other options.

The sad part is that no one who knew me suspected that I had these feelings, because I became a master at wearing my mask. I showed up for work every day, worked hard, and took care of my children. I dressed neatly, made people laugh, and my marriage was envied by female coworkers. From the outside looking in, why would I consider taking my life? After all, I had it all!

Masks come in all shapes and sizes. Some with makeup, and others in their natural state. As women, we use many things to cover up hurt, betrayal and trauma, and we believe that we are effectively concealing what is going on inside. We develop unhealthy habits such as overeating, substance abuse, excessive shopping, and other self-injurious behaviors. I became a workaholic. If there was overtime to be had, I was your girl. Work was the safest place for me during those years, so anytime there was a chance to stay later, I jumped on it. However, my finances were not under my control, since everything I made was taken by my husband.

> *When I verbalized the abuse in safe spaces, my support team was loving, patient and proactive.*

There were times when a sense of dread came over me at the end of the week. I knew that the weekend did not afford me the opportunity to be out of the house, at least not without my husband, or one of his family members that he had keeping an "eye" on me. I never knew what kind of mood he would be in, or what me or the kids would do to set him off. Although the kids were not physically abused, I learned later that children are affected emotionally when there is abuse in the home. He never hit me in front of the kids. However, there were times when they could hear me crying, but were too little to understand what was going on. I am sure that the nervous energy I gave off while at home was felt by them as well. This was when I realized that it was time to be open and tell someone about the abuse.

Thankfully, courage finally showed up! I received support from my mom and you know what? She never once told me that I was stupid. She immediately sprang into action to assist me in devising an exit plan. It was like a weight had been lifted off my shoulders! When I verbalized the abuse in safe spaces, my support team was loving, patient and proactive.

Now, with a newfound confidence and hope, naivety reared its ugly head. I actually believed that getting out of the violent environment was as simple as saying these three words, "*I am leaving*!"

The day I told my husband I was tired of living in an abusive marriage, and that I wanted to leave with my children, was one of the scariest days of my life. I had rehearsed my speech to him repeatedly, along with trying to prepare myself for his responses. I called my mother down to our apartment, as she lived within walking distance, and she came to be there with me as I delivered the news.

Initially, my husband appeared to be shocked at the fact that I decided to leave. He said things like, "I cannot believe you are doing this," and, "How can you break up our family like this?" Then he begged me to stay one more night and talk things through without my mother being there. He always hated the fact that my mother was around, because out of everyone he isolated me from, my mother would not stay away. His begging and pleading went on for over an hour, and it finally wore me down to the point that I told my mother I would stay and hear him out.

Now, this is the part of the story like in all suspense movies where you are yelling at the screen, "***GIRL! GET OUT!***" However, I did not leave with my mother and children. I stayed to hear what he had to say, and I made up my mind that I was going to leave the next day and never look back. I am not sure why I felt that I owed him that, but I did it anyway. Looking back, I think I was looking for a glimmer of hope that things could be better, that he would finally change now that he saw my willingness to leave.

So, we began to talk, just the two of us, and he was trying to plead his case as to why I needed to stay. He brought up every great thing he ever did over the course of our marriage. Of course, he did not speak about the times in which he hurt me so bad that I could not go to work, or the time I didn't have full range of motion of my right arm, because he slammed a door on it to keep me from leaving. No, he did not talk about the times when I was forced to remain nude, or in very little clothing while at home, because he felt that this was a way to keep me from reaching out to the neighbors for help when he attacked me. He attempted to paint the most glorious picture he could, so that I would doubt myself and ultimately remain in the home. Through every attempt to convince me to stay, I stood my ground and remained resolute in my decision to leave.

The conversation went on well into the night, with him pleading and me standing firm in my decision. Before we knew it, the sun was starting to rise, and I was exhausted, as I had not slept all night. I knew I had to get ready for work in a few hours. The last plea he made for me to stay was unsuccessful, and then the mood of the conversation shifted. His voice changed, and his demeanor became dark and threatening.

His affect was flat, and he asked, "So, you're not going to stay?"

"No, I can't do this any longer," I exclaimed, "Love is not supposed to hurt!"

His voice became menacing and he said, "Well, if you do not want to stay, the only way you will leave is in a body bag!"

At that moment, I knew I was in trouble. His eyes showed nothing in them, and his face had an angry expression. He grabbed me and began choking me. I struggled to push him off of me, but he had a firm grip around my neck. All I could think of was that my kids were going to grow up without me, and that this could have been avoided if I had left with my mother the night before.

I managed to get away from him long enough to run into the kitchen, but he was right behind me, and began choking me from behind. This time, I had no way to get him off of me.

We were by the kitchen sink, and laying on the sink was a hammer. I do not know what came over me, but I grabbed that hammer and I hit him in the elbow with the side that you use to pull nails out of wood! When I did that, he let go of me, and ran out of the apartment. I fell to the floor crying and trying to catch my breath with the hammer still in my hand.

Once I was able to collect myself, I called my mother on the phone and screamed for her to come down there immediately! I was so shaken; I did not know what to do. I did not call the police. I just got out of there!

Later that day, I spoke to my coworker's husband, who was a police officer, and told him what happened. However, I refused to press charges. He provided me with information on how I could safely leave the residence, which was what I wanted to do. My family made sure that I was packed up and moved within days of the incident. I was blessed to be able to move to an undisclosed location that was over 45 minutes from where we lived, and I stayed there until I was able to secure a place of my own. Coming to and going from work was like an undercover operation, as I had to be careful to make sure I was not followed. This went on for over a year, until we were officially divorced, and he moved on to another woman.

After four years of being single, along came my second husband, and I really thought he was the one. You see, my self-esteem was so poor that I was glad that someone showed me affection. I went from a father who I felt rejected me, to a husband who beat me physically, mentally, and emotionally. So, to have a man show the least bit of interest in me, was wonderful!

After getting married for the second time, I had my youngest daughter. Although my second husband did not beat me with his fists, mentally and emotionally, I was beat up like an opponent in the boxing ring with Mike Tyson.

We were both toxic for each other, as I had not healed from the trauma experienced in my first marriage, and I allowed it to spill over into my second marriage, to the point that I became the aggressor. My thought process was that I would never allow anyone to abuse me again. It became clear that neither one of us was ready for marriage. He had never been married, and had a list of insecurities of his own, along with some other addictive habits.

After three years, this marriage ended in divorce, and it took what little self-esteem I had with it. This time, there was an outward manifestation, such as not doing my hair, not ironing my clothes, and becoming easily irritated. I was in a dark place and I did not know how to get out of it. I was ashamed, and felt like a failure to

have been through two marriages, only to end up

alone. I did not share my

The journey of self-discovery yielded some good fruit.

story with anyone, as the

thought of hearing those

words out loud made me

physically ill. I did not seek counseling, because I

was not aware that this was something people

went to counselors for. I thought I needed to

toughen up and get over it. I had kids who needed

me, as well as a mom, so there was no time to feel

sorry for myself.

I have been divorced for the second time for

20 years now, and throughout those years, I have

taken a personal journey to get to know ME. I

wanted to know what Alicia liked, who she wanted

to be, and how she could turn her pain into purpose.

The journey of self-discovery yielded some good fruit. I was introduced to the Lord, and entered into a relationship with Christ. Through my walk with Christ, I found that there was a strong, capable woman inside of me, and my circumstances did not dictate my destiny.

I also did the necessary work on myself, connecting with individuals who were positive, spirit-filled, and intentional about helping women connect with their purpose by facing their past, and speaking life into their present. I had to change my perspective, confessions, and actions.

At times, our healing from past hurts is delayed because we continue to resurrect dead things, such as relationships, events, and situations, with our conversations. I had to learn how to change the way I viewed and communicated what I experienced, using it to bless others and assist them in their journey towards healing.

> *I encourage you to tear down the memorials and monuments you have set up with your words...*

I went back to school when my youngest daughter was two-months-old, and pursued my bachelor's degree. Then, when she was in middle school, I went back to school to obtain my Master's degree, and now I am currently in school working on my PhD. I am a licensed counselor and have a better understanding of who I am and what I am worth.

I encourage you to tear down the memorials and monuments you have set up with your words through the eyes of a victim. Now when I tell my story, I share with people that I am not just a survivor of domestic violence, I. Am. A. CHAMPION! Every time I share my story, I reclaim a piece of me. As a Christian and a therapist, my desire is to promote the health and welfare of the whole human family. Domestic violence affects entire families; Women are abused, kids are stressed, confused, and afraid, and the cycle can repeat itself if the appropriate interventions are not made.

If you or someone you know is currently involved in a violent relationship, please reach out to your local domestic violence agencies, or the national domestic violence hotline for assistance. If you have experienced trauma of any kind and need someone to talk to, please reach out to therapists in your area. Psychology Today is a magazine that can be accessed from the internet. You can also reach out to your benefit carrier through your employer. Most employers offer Employee Assistance Programs (EAP) and those services are free for the first few visits.

As stated previously, I pray that my story will be instrumental in your ability to live courageously. Wearing masks to cover up hurt, disappointment, and failure can become cumbersome. Once you put the mask on, you must work hard at keeping it on to avoid people seeing you with all your flaws and insecurities. Like I said earlier, masks come in all forms...for some women it is expensive clothing, jewelry, and makeup. For others, it is toxic relationships, because the

> *...make the conscious decision that you are WORTHY, and no mask can cover that up.*

thought of having a significant other is better than being alone, and this further perpetuates the façade. I challenge you to take an honest reflective view of yourself, and make the conscious decision that you are WORTHY, and no mask can cover that up.

No matter what your life has been up to this point, you can pivot and change directions. We have what we speak. To change your outcome, you must change your confession. Go out and be bold and courageous, while making memorable moments here on earth.

Throughout my journey, and in an attempt to change what I spoke over myself, the following poem came to me as I was preparing for a speaking engagement. I wanted to share this with the hopes that it would encourage those who read it.

Woman of Worth, God's Masterpiece

Hey, look at you, so stylish and full of grace

You enter a room with such poise, as the light
beams on your face

As the crowd turns to see what all the fuss is about

Although trying to hide, your radiance stands out

Assurance and confidence are unspoken words

Whispers and questions are all that is heard

Who is she? Where did she come from?

How did she get here and who is she with?

YOU, my dear are a Woman of Worth

And do not ever forget!

Alicia P. Harris MA LPC LAC NCC

Connect with Alicia

Phone: (803) 814-4011

Facebook:
https://www.facebook.com/brellacounselingservices

LinkedIn: http://linkedin.com/in/alicia-harris-ma-lpc-lac-ncc-2a788444

Email: brellaservicesllc@gmail.com

About The Author

Carolyn Allen

Carolyn Allen is a minister at a local church, in North Carolina. She is a graduate of the Carolina College of Biblical Studies, with a degree in Biblical Studies, and a minor in Biblical Counseling.

Carolyn founded a nonprofit women's ministry in October 2016, called Women of Conversation. Women of Conversation targets women who have been broken by years of embedded pain, traumas and tragedies. Women who have been told for years that they would never be nothing, never amount to nothing, and would never produce nothing.

Women of Conversation teaches women to use every negative word as a stepping stone into their "DESTINY" by proclaiming through the word what God says, and through the scripture which brings them on a journey from "PAIN TO PRAISE".

Carolyn grew up, in Fort Lauderdale, Florida, and currently resides in a small town in North Carolina, along with her husband and daughter. Carolyn is a mother of three, and a grandmother of two. She enjoys singing, taking long trips, and spending quality time, with her family.

Read along on Carolyn's journey as her prayer and faith in God delivers her premature baby girl into a healthy, well-adjusted teenager...Her Joi!

RISING JOI

By

Carolyn Allen

I just knew I had the perfect life. I just knew our love would last forever. So much for forever, because there I was, after 14 years of marriage, with two boys, ages ten and five, lost and alone. I felt empty. I was losing hope. I felt lifeless, and my joy was gone.

My husband and I had made a vow, for better or for worse, for richer or poorer, in sickness and in health, till death do us part. But that was not how it ended. Although, we did have a good start.

I remember it like it was yesterday. I walked across the stage, at Dillard High School, June 1982, and received my high school diploma. One week later, I kissed my mom and dad goodbye, and headed to North Carolina with my high school sweetheart.

We were married one month later, in July, and I became pregnant in August. In May 1983, my baby boy was born, weighing 8 pounds 15 ounces. He was all a mother could dream of! He was healthy, and yes, he came out hungry! He had ten fingers and ten toes. I was told that was the first thing to check.

All my life, as far as I could remember, I wanted to be a nurse. After my son turned three, I planned to go back to school. This was very hard for me, because I was a stay-at-home mom, and my son was very attached to me. Every time I would take him to the sitter, he would cry, but we managed to get through it.

I went back to school in August 1984. As soon as I finished all of my prerequisite courses, I became pregnant with my second son. He was five years apart from his brother, and he weighed 6 pounds 2 ounces. Although he was smaller than his older brother, he was a much busier baby. I had to place my schooling on hold once again, to raise my sons.

You see, I married a soldier, and oftentimes, as a soldier's wife, my career was put on hold to support his career, especially because we had young children. My life revolved around his, and this ended up causing a strain on our marriage.

We had many ups and downs, misunderstandings, and miscommunication along the way. He would have to have it his way, or I would have to have it my way, and the enemy declared that the winner would be divorce, and that was the final blow.

Divorce came with a price. It was 1995, and I was so broken and busted on the inside. My dreams were shattered. I was lonely and empty, and it took my breath away at times. I was disconnected from the world. I looked pretty on the outside, but I was cut up and bleeding on the inside. I was suffering in silence, because my momma taught me to "never let them see you sweat".

Years later, in 1997, I met a young man who had a story, not like mine, but one all his own. He was in love with his college sweetheart. They were preparing for marriage, and the plans fell apart. I was hurting and so was he. I remember crying all night on the phone and being soothed by his voice telling me, "Don't cry. Everything's going to be alright."

This man eventually asked me to marry him, but I did not know what I wanted. All I knew was, I did not want to be hurt again. I was still dealing with my past hurt, and did not want another marriage that "looked" like it would be forever. So, I told him no, and he waited, and waited, and waited.

During this time, I had made up my mind to turn away from the world, and turn back to God. This would be the turning point in my life. Don't get me wrong, I had some good times when I was out in the world. I would party at Pope Air Force Base until they turned the lights on, and at Fort Bragg, when they would turn on the lights and say, "You ain't got to go home, but you got to get out of here." And let's not forget the NCO Club in Bamberg, Germany. Those were the days, I thought.

I must admit, that the path I wrote for my life was not all that bad, it just was not the one God had written for me. Jeremiah 29:11 says, "For I know the plans I have for you," declares the Lord, "plans to prosper you and not to harm you, plans to give you hope and a future."

In February 2001, I finally said yes to this loving and caring man that waited for me! He even recommitted his life to Christ. He is my best friend, and we love God and each other. He makes me smile and laugh uncontrollably. I even got my joy back!

Two years later, in 2003, I had his child. We had a girl and her middle name is Joi. She was born prematurely at 26 weeks, due to a large fibroid in my uterus. She weighed only two pounds and seven ounces when she was born, and had to stay in the Neonatal Intensive Care Unit for 48 days.

During this time, her daddy prayed Psalms chapter 23 over her every morning. Afterwards, I would sing Blessed Assurance to her. Joi was a fighter. Every time I would walk near her incubator, she would immediately fasten her right eye on me. She'd have her head bowed, face down, with her left eye sunken, in the mattress pad, but her right eye was focused directly on me. She had a seeing eye, and paid close attention to my comings and goings. When she sensed that I was getting closer to her, her inhaling and exhaling would become more pronounced. Her nurse, Anthony, would say, "You going to need, to buy that sista some patent leather shoes, because she's going to be the boss."

Joi was dedicated to the Lord in November 2003. She squirmed in the pastor's hand the whole time. It was so funny how the people laughed, as she had her way that day.

Joi had a playful side. She started walking at eight months old. I remember lying in bed, watching as she stood up trying to run, and then fell down. When she was eighteen months, she would stand behind me, wrap her tiny arms around my leg, hug it tightly, and then giggle and run away.

Joi always walked on her tippy toes. I followed my dad's advice and enrolled her in ballet classes. She loved to make noise as well, and she made much as she could, usually singing into the microphone of her first piano. Joi loved to sing.

Today, nearly eighteen years later, she still loves to dance, and up until the COVID-19 pandemic occurred, she was enrolled in high school

dance every year. She still loves to sing, especially

in the church choir, which she has been a part of

since age five and she sings with such grace.

She is a high school senior, graduating in

the class of 2021. She is bossy, and has outgrown

those patent leather shoes. She still has a keen eye,

and she is my "Rising Joi".

Connect with Carolyn

Email: womenofconversation2911@gmail.com

About The Author

Charlotte Cowser

Charlotte Cowser was born in South Ruislip, England, United Kingdom, while her father was stationed at Chicksand Air Force Base.

Being raised in a military family, and previously married to military men, she'd traveled to a few countries, and lived in a variety of different states, before settling in Atlanta, Georgia, for 18 years.

She relocated to Sacramento, California, as a Regional Manager for a major moving company, and to be near her aging parents.

Charlotte retired from that company, and a few years later, started her non-profit organization, Sloan Selective Services Inc., which focuses on the outplacement and lifestyles of seniors through physical and mental activities. Charlotte provides snacks for the homeless in her spare time.

Follow along as Charlotte goes from a Silver Spoon upbringing, through an unexpected journey, and learns valuable life lessons along the way.

SILVER SPOON

By

Charlotte Cowser

I grew up in a military family. My father was a retired Chief Master Sergeant in the United States Air Force. My mother was outgoing, strong-willed, and glamorous. My mother played the piano, and she could sing. Her voice was so beautiful! She loved her four daughters.

She would always say, "Don't take any wooden nickels," and, "Don't date men that wear blue jeans and sneakers," and, "Never let a man put his hands on you."

My first husband was a suit and tie man in the Air Force. He was stationed at the Pentagon, and we lived in Virginia. Our marriage lasted five years, then ended, due to his infidelity and the fact that he decided to give me my first black eye. He hit me so hard my retina tore. When we went to the hospital and the doctor asked what happened, I actually said my two-year-old son accidentally kicked me in my eye. I could see in his face that he did not believe me.

I called my husband's First Sergeant, and had him removed from the home. Until I could get on my feet, they gave me two weeks before I needed to be moved out of base housing. I found a studio apartment that I could afford, and filed for a divorce about a year or so later.

I decided not to date for a few years and focus merely on my children. I met my second husband in 1987. He was a blue jeans and sneakers man, and he was in the United States Army. My daughter was born while my second husband and I were stationed in Germany. My husband was so excited when she was born. She was daddy's little girl, and it was love at first sight.

In August 1992, the Army put my husband out for not qualifying to move on to his next stripe. We decided to settle in Atlanta, Georgia. Around March of 1998, I noticed a change in my husband. He was not spending as much time with our daughter as he normally did. When she would ask him questions, he would say, "Ask your mother," and he was going out more often than usual. To be honest, before my husband's behavioral change, he spent more time with his daughter than I did.

I was an undercover workaholic. Then, the company I was with merged with another company, and had to close their stores, and I lost my job. We were now on one salary and had to move out of our four-bedroom home to a rented, small, starter home, and then from the starter home to a rented townhome. Within a three-year span, we also had to downside from two cars to one.

One day, my husband came home and told me some devastating news.

"I have a problem," he said.

I asked, "What is the problem?"

He said, "I'm using cocaine."

"You need to stop!" I yelled. "You have a family to take care of!"

He walked out of the door saying, "I'll be back."

I was in denial about how bad this was. I hid his addiction from friends, family, and my children.

How was I going to get my husband back to reality, when I had no clue myself what was happening?

Once my husband walked out the door, he did not return until a few days later. One thing I have never done was argue in front of the children, and I was not going start tonight. We needed to have this conversation at the right time and in the right place.

I had a revolving door marriage. He would come home as if we were going to work out our problems together, and then after a few weeks, go back to the other woman, and continue to use his drug of choice...cocaine. I would allow this for several months until I had enough.

I woke up one morning thinking my husband had gotten a ride to work, because his car was still parked outside. However, when I looked in the closets, most of his clothes were gone. I sat down and talked with my daughter and told her that her dad has a problem, and he needed to get help. She began to cry, and say that he did not love her. I tried to explain to her that his actions were not her fault, but she did not believe me. Hell, I did not even believe myself.

I eventually found out he moved in with another woman. She was the mother of two daughters, and their father had custody.

I went into survival mode. I needed a job...any job. I was mentally living in a cloud of disbelief. I had no money at all, and very little food. I was wondering how the rent, utilities, and car payment would be made.

I got up early the next morning, determined and desperate to find a job. When I went in the closet to look for something nice to wear, I found that all my nice clothes and coats had been cut up.

Then I heard my daughter ask, "Mom, how am I getting to school?"

I looked out the window, and the car was gone! The repo man had taken my car! I tried calling my husband at work, but he was not there. I asked one of my husband's co-workers, one who I knew was close to him, to come by. My 17-year-old son had ridden with a friend to school. I took on the task of getting my daughter to school.

When the friend arrived, I told him what had been going on, and that we needed help. I needed food and bus fare so that I could find a job.

He took me to the store for food, bought me a newspaper, and gave me $40. I salvaged what I could of my clothes, and in the pouring cold and rain, with a plastic bag as my scarf, and a trash bag as my coat, I walked to the bus station. Being brought up with a silver spoon in my mouth, I had never ridden public transportation before. I felt like I was no longer in control of my life. I was needy.

I landed a job as a Produce Clerk at Wayfield Foods in East Point, Georgia. I caught rides to the food bank and Goodwill. I hated my husband. By this time, he had officially stopped all communication with our daughter.

My daughter was now a teenager with a lot of built-up emotional pain, disappointment, and confusion. She still felt responsible for her father's behavior.

We had moved again. I found another job closer to home, and my daughter's school was within walking distance. I bought a hooptie to get around in.

One day, my daughter called me at work crying. She said she was depressed, and did not want to live. She felt like everything happening between her father and I was her fault. I cannot put into words what hearing this did to me. This was my breaking point emotionally. I told her I was coming home.

I contacted a family friend that she looked up to like an uncle, and told him what she said. He agreed to meet me at the house. I felt like I was living in a nightmare that would never end. We had gone from a loving family, to a roller-coaster ride. This was the transformation of our lives.

I had to be strong. I acted like things were going to be okay for my children, but deep down, I knew I needed to figure out how I was going to save my daughter.

I sat outside of my house, waiting for her uncle. I could not go in alone I chanted, "*Be strong. Don't cry. Be strong. Don't cry.*"

When we entered the house, she was in her room. Her uncle called for her to come out and join us in the living room. As I looked into my daughter's eyes, I was literally shaking. I tried my best not to shed a tear. Her eyes were swollen from crying. She rubbed her eyes and continued to cry.

Her uncle asked her what was going on. She told him that she was depressed and had been for a while. When he asked her how she knew this, she told him that she had looked up the way she was feeling on the Internet, and she had all the symptoms: feelings of sadness, tearfulness, hopelessness, feelings of worthlessness, and that she didn't want to live. She told him that everything was her fault.

As I did many times through the years I opened up and managed to say, "Your dad loves you. He has a problem, and he needs to help himself. As your mother, I need to help you."

Tears started to fall from my face, and my breathing got heavy.

"If you feel like hurting yourself," I said, "Then I don't know what else to do but call someplace to confine you immediately...hospital, police, child services. I love you so much, and the only way I can protect you is to protect you from hurting yourself. I cannot work and provide for us knowing your feelings."

We cried together and hugged each other tightly. When I felt her arms around me, I knew we would get through this. A few months had passed with no episodes of depression, and we had conversations every day.

Then at 16, my daughter got a boyfriend. He was 17, from Stone Mountain, Georgia, and was being raised by his grandmother. We lived in Decatur, Georgia, at the time, in a place that I could afford raising two children on my own.

One night, while I was sleeping, I heard a noise coming from my daughter's room. She'd had a couple of her girlfriends from school spending the night. I looked out my window and there was a dark black SUV with the lights dim. I knew her boyfriend did not have a car, and I could not see who the driver was.

As I walked toward her room, I heard unfamiliar voices. My first thought was, *Hell no*! I grabbed the bat and busted through the door, swinging the bat and cussing! Her boyfriend flew out of her bedroom window, breaking the glass. The other young man went behind him. I called the girlfriends' parents first to advise of what had happened, and to ask them to come and pick up their daughters.

I asked my daughter who was in the SUV. She said it was her boyfriend's uncle.

I said, "We will be at your boyfriend's house in the morning. I will be letting his grandmother know he is not welcomed at my house anymore."

When we arrived the next morning, his grandmother met us outside. She was a very well-dressed woman. Silver spoon raised, or so it seemed. She stated her grandson had already told her what happened, and he was not hurt from jumping through the window. She also said he had been advised to stay away from lower class girls from Decatur, and that he knows better. Let's just say, if my daughter was not with me, I'm not sure what the outcome would have been.

My daughter was now focused on graduating high school with a dual diploma, and a 4.0 GPA. She had landed a job working at AMC Movie Theaters, and had gotten a car. Meanwhile, a young man kept showing up at her job and asking her out. She told me she was not interested in him, but over time, his persistence won, and she gave him her information. The young man wanted to come to the house to visit her. I agreed, because it was time for this mom to find out what's this young man was all about.

He was in college, but had dropped out. Then he worked as an usher at Creflo Dollar's church, but said they fired him for no reason. His mother did not drive, so he took her to work at Kroger's, and she lived with him.

"I really like your daughter," he said.

My daughter didn't seem too interested in our conversation.

Now it was 2007, and it was time for me to get my daughter settled at Clayton State College. I was sad to have my baby girl leave home, but glad we were at this point in our journey. I would go by her apartment, maybe once a week to check in. A couple of times when she should have been studying, I noticed her boyfriend was there.

I asked her, "Why is he always here?"

"He's not really, Mom," she said. "His mother's boyfriend moved in, so he comes here to relax."

"I hope you are taking your birth control pills," I said.

"Don't worry Mom," she said. "He said he is sterile."

I didn't have a good feeling about this. One Saturday, I decided to go by her job and see a movie. When I pulled into the parking lot next to her car, eggs were all over the front windshield.

I went inside her job and asked, "What happened to your car?"

"I don't know Mom," she said. "When my boyfriend walked me to the car this morning, this is what we found. It may have been one of his exes."

"He let you drive to work with splattered egg on your windshield," I asked. "Why didn't he clean it up? I will take your car and get it washed."

"No Mom. He said he will do it when I get off," she said.

I went to my car and called her boyfriend, and told him to meet me in the Auto Zone parking lot. I had a brief discussion with him about responsibility, accountability and support. His response was very defensive.

Later that evening my daughter called me. With not even a hello, she asked, "What did you say to my boyfriend?"

"Hold on wait!" I exclaimed. "I am your mother. Watch your tone!"

This was our first disagreement. I knew this guy was no good! I would have to back up and back out, and play his game in order to keep my daughter from his love spell.

One day, I came home from work, and there was a note on my bed that said *"To Mom"*. I quickly opened it up, and it read:

Dear Mom, please don't disown me and think I am a disappointment. I know you wanted me to finish college, but I'm pregnant.

I dropped to my knees, and must have cried for two hours clenching the note. I called her dad and told him.

"What are you so upset about," he asked. "She is grown."

I quickly disconnected the call. What really hurt was that she thought I would ever disown her, or be disappointed in her, I went to her college apartment, and told her I would never have those feelings.

"I love you," I said, "But how could you get pregnant if he said he could not have children?"

A few months later they got an apartment. She stopped going to college. I made my visits scarce, all the while thinking he has won.

An opportunity came up on my job to transfer to California. Having lived in Georgia for 18 years, and with my son now living in China, I kept thinking how do I leave my daughter? If I stay, will we grow apart because of him? I can't bear to lose my daughter over this creep.

After much thought, I requested the transfer to relocate to California. My U-Haul dealers picked up my U-Haul. There was a gas shortage everywhere at this time, but I found a gas station, gassed up my 17-foot truck, and packed and loaded it with my car attached.

My daughter was there, and I asked her, "Are you sure you don't want to go?"

"No Mom. We will be fine," she said.

We laid on the floor in the bare house and talked, hugged, and nodded off to sleep, until it was time for me to get on the road to California. It was so hard to leave her, but it was for the best.

Shortly before my granddaughter was born, my daughter and her boyfriend got married. I flew back for the birth of the baby.

Now I'm a grandma, and flying back for my granddaughter's first birthday. I made sure I had my own hotel, as my son-in-law did not seem like he wanted to stick around when I was town. He would come in quietly, kiss my daughter on the cheek, and leave again. Sometimes, the trash can would be running over. Why can't this dude at least take out the trash?

While my granddaughter enjoyed her nap time, my daughter and I decided to relax and enjoy some time together. On the countertop, I noticed a cut-off notice from Georgia Power. I did not comment on it. I sat on the couch next to her, and we laughed and talked.

Then my daughter said, "Mom let me show you some cute girl's clothes. I'll just use my husband's laptop instead of getting up for mine."

The laptop was on coffee table next to her. As she was looking for the website, she hollered loudly, then tears started falling down her face. I moved closer to her to see what was wrong. Oh my God! Here was my son-in-law posing half-naked on a website for big juicy women. Some messages were from dates he had been on with one lady, who asked him if he thought his wife would join in?

Just as I was trying to comfort her, and tell her to pack her shit because she and my granddaughter were coming home with me, my son-in-law walked in. My daughter flew from the couch towards him! I tried to grab her, but I fell backward. I pulled her off of him, and she ran into the bedroom. I opened the laptop and showed him why she was so upset, and let him know they were coming with me.

He said, "I'm going to talk to my wife."

"Not by yourself you're not," I said. "You can talk to her in front of me."

I went into the room where she was sitting in disbelief, and asked, "Do you want to speak to him?"

There was some hesitation, then she walked out the room with me and sat down.

I advised her, "Don't attack him anymore. Think of your daughter in the other room sleeping."

I went back into the other room, and heard him say, "You stopped giving me attention like you used to. Please don't leave me."

He began sniffling as if he was crying, and he said, "Just let me tell you something. Nobody knows I was raped by an uncle growing up. My mom dates men that use her. I never got any attention."

I wanted to come out the room and beat his ass myself. After moments of silence I walked out the room. My daughter was distraught. He was standing and wiping his face.

I asked my daughter again, "Are you coming with me? I leave in two days, and need to get tickets. You can leave everything behind."

"No Mom," she said, "I am going to work through this with him."

Five months later, I get a call from my daughter.

"Mom, we are coming to California to stay with you until we get settled. Everyone is coming."

I couldn't say no but hopefully, things would be changing for the better. I set them up with a 10-foot U-Haul truck for them to make the move.

Once my daughter and her family came to live with me, several things were obvious and noticeable. We all had job except her husband. I had been storing my son's belongings, books, video games, and gaming systems in my closet. One day, I decided to clean out the closet and move my son's things in my garage to provide more room for my daughter and son-in-law's belongings. When I opened the closet, there was no gaming system, and the video games were gone.

I asked my son in law about this and he denied knowing anything saying, "I would never steal from the hand that's helping us out."

I sat down with my daughter and explained where I stored her brother's stuff. She went in protective mode for her husband, saying, "If he said he didn't know anything, I believe him."

I advised my daughter that he was not going to lay around while she and I were at work. He had two weeks to get a job or he was moving back to Georgia.

He said he had a job at 24-Hour Fitness. My gut kept saying that was a lie. After he went to work, I arrived there at 6am, and looked around for him. I noticed a worker at a desk, who turned out to be the manager. I asked for my son-in-law by name.

The manager said, "No one works here by that name."

I described my son-in-law.

"I did not hire him," the manager said. "He was very interesting. He asked me if I could give him a gym shirt so he could show he had a job!"

I went home and decided to wait to tell my daughter when her and her husband were both together, so there would be no misunderstanding as to why I was sending him back to Georgia.

I setup a meeting with my daughter and her husband, and I explained to my daughter that he faked having a job. I let her know that it was time to put him on the midnight bus to Georgia. I offered him some money, but he declined. Later, I found out why. When I got home, I discovered that my money in my wallet was gone!

As time passed, my daughter and I had an ok relationship, but it was not as close as it had been before this man entered her life. She would up getting her own apartment and car. She let me know her husband was coming back so they could live as a family.

I asked her why and she said, "Mom, I don't want to end up like you did...a struggling single mom."

My daughter and her family moved into a duplex. She got a job working for the State of California, and as a Zumba fitness instructor. One day, I got a call from her saying, "Mom, you better come over here. I'm going to hurt him!"

I was there in less than three minutes. When I arrived, he was getting some of his things together to leave.

My granddaughter walked up to me and said, "Mommy broke my window. She threw something at daddy."

I took my granddaughter in her room and sat and talked with her. I saw the broken window and thought it was a good thing that it was a double-paned window.

I went to speak to my daughter, and she told me that my granddaughter was sitting on the couch next to her dad. She had asked her dad if she could she play on his phone to look at videos, and then she saw her dad with another man and women at their old apartment about to perform sexual acts!

I needed to take a moment to breathe. Even as I am writing this, the anger, pain, resentment are still there. At the time, all I could do was hug my daughter tight as she cried. Who knows what all my granddaughter had seen her father do?

I asked my daughter if she considered having him locked up because what my granddaughter saw was a form of child abuse. I reminded her that she was a good wife and mother. I asked my daughter to seek counseling, and to talk to someone at her job in Human Resources about a counseling referral. I could now see the signs of depression. She would cry at a drop of a dime, and became distant. I could not lose my daughter to this creep!

My daughter informed me that my son-in-law was going to counseling for sex addiction. The therapist would begin working with him, and eventually, she would have to come in for a session. I was not buying this. It sounded like another lie, and another opportunity for him to control her.

She said, "Mom let's just see what happens. Dad was an addict, and now I'm married to an addict!"

She let him move back in after a few weeks. A few more weeks passed by, and I get a call from my daughter asking me to pick up my granddaughter. Her voice sounded strange and somewhat shaken. Later that evening I asked what was going on?

She said, "He's in jail."

"What," I asked.

"The sheriff picked him up this afternoon at the house, and left pictures of where they had been following him," she said. "They took his electronic devices."

"For what," I asked.

She said, "He is being accused of having sex with a minor. Her face blushed red, and her eyes darkened. She was in limbo. I could feel it see it, and she looked like she was denial about the situation.

We went to the first two hearings. Bail was set at $500.000. When my daughter heard the father of the victim speak about how he trusted my son-in-law because he had helped him lose weight as a personal trainer, saved his life, and how he thought they were friends, she was all choked up.

The father continued speaking to the judge saying, "I decided to have him train my 15-year-old daughter, and instead of training her, he was sleeping with her."

Not to my surprise, my daughter's car payments that my son-in-law was to pay, were in default, and the utility bills were on payment arrangements. I paid her bills up, and made her car payments, until emotionally she could see clearly, until she could see her worth. I wanted her to know

162

that she could be a single mom, and love her daughter for her own survival if need be.

We stopped going to the hearings, and her self-healing started. He was convicted to six years in prison, and had to register as a sex offender. I advised my daughter that it was time to take all the necessary legal steps, so that she could heal and move on with her and your daughter's future. She needed to free herself, and do an emotional amputation from this toxic relationship of deception. She needed to take her life back.

Within months, she filed for full custody and a divorce, and went back to college. She bought a vehicle in cash, and got promoted on her job to a supervisor, and she solely supported herself and her daughter.

163

A year later, she met and got engaged to a man who loves her for her, understands her journey, respects her, and loves and treats my granddaughter as his own.

I never thought that being raised with a silver spoon, meant that you're too good for real life lessons. I learned in writing this chapter that I buried my own hurt and pain, and suppressed a lot of emotions along the way. We forgave her dad, and we hold no grudges. We are free!

Update:

Remember my daughter's first boyfriend in Atlanta? Years later, he murdered his next girlfriend! He is currently serving life in prison.

My ex-husband went to rehab. He is a few years sober, and married to the woman from his addiction years.

My daughter's ex-husband is currently out on parole, with an ankle bracelet, and registered as a sex offender. He has supervised visits with my granddaughter.

I started my own non-profit business, Sloan Selective Services Inc, and I'm taking a college course in Sociology. I am happily living single.

Connect with Charlotte

Email: sloanselectiveservicesinc@gmail.com

About The Author

Onita V. Simpson

Onita Simpson is a mother to two teenage daughters. She served in the Army for almost nine years, and during that time, she deployed to Afghanistan for one year.

After departing the Army, she received her Bachelor of Science degree in Criminal Justice from

Campbell University in 2011, and her Masters of Arts in Human Resource Development from Webster University.

She has been a paraprofessional, working in the government sector for over 20 years. She owns an online clothing store that she uses to empower and encourage women and men to combine fashion with words.

Onita is also a motivational speaker, and she enjoys writing in her leisure time. Read along as Onita shares how her faith in God, despite her trials, restored her to a place of absolute Redemption!

RE-DEMP-TION

By

Onita V. Simpson

I was sound asleep in my warm bed in the stillness of the early morning, when I was grabbed from behind! Someone was hugging and holding me tightly, and it gave me a sense of fear! I quickly realized it was my husband, but I was confused by this gesture. I could feel his heart beating so fast against my back!

"Are you ok?" I asked.

"I had a dream that everything was gone. You the girls, and the furniture," he said. "The only thing that was left was this bed."

I can't lie...I was glad we were laying in the dark, so he couldn't see the smirk on my face. I immediately thought, *that's going to be true if you don't get yourself together*.

We had accomplished so much together that I just knew I was living "the dream". We purchased our first home at the age of 26. I was in college, as well as being active duty in the Army. He was also doing well in the Army. We were both hands-on parents with our two young daughters, and we can't leave out the dog! I had what I had always wanted...a family.

In 2011, after being married for a little over eight years, I realized that we were no longer on the same path. We had come to a fork in the road, and would have to decide if we wanted to continue on this journey together, or choose our separate routes. The warning of that dream would start to unfold into our reality just two years later.

I graduated with my Bachelor's degree in Criminal Justice in June 2011. After that, nothing was ever the same. My husband had been stationed to the Midwest, in Iowa, while the girls and I remained in South Carolina. I was no longer in the Army, and in a few months, after graduation, I would be giving up my job to move to the Midwest, so our family unit could be back together.

School was about to start, and we needed to get the girls settled into their new home. My husband picked a home that he thought was suitable for us to rent. I took some time off from work so that we could drive 13 hours to the Midwest and get settled in our new home.

Once we got there, I was able to see the home for the first time. As I walked through the house, I kept telling myself, *This is good. This will be fine.* Meanwhile, I had the worst feeling in my gut that this was far from good.

My eyes zoomed in on the layers of dust and pet dander on the blinds. I immediately thought of our youngest daughter, who suffers from allergies to just about everything, and the fact that she would have to live here. My nostrils flared at the smell of pet urine. But this could be fixed, right? I felt an uneasiness about this situation, but allowed the movers to continue bringing in furniture. An hour into moving our furniture in, I smelled one more whiff of cat urine, and it set me off!

"STOP! Don't move anything else into this house," I told the movers. I just couldn't do it. This couldn't be where we would be living. This was not a suitable home for our children or for me. I demanded the number to the landlord to address my concerns about the home not being ready as promised, and to request our deposit back. The landlord didn't argue or try and make any concessions.

He simply said, "We'll have a check ready for you tomorrow." Clearly, he knew he was wrong.

Now that that was taken care of, what were we going to do about this furniture that had been moved in? The Army had paid for our household goods to be moved to the new home, and once they move them into the dwelling, they aren't

authorized to remove them again without a

contract. I literally sat out on the curb lost, and

homeless. The home we thought we were going to

live in wasn't in livable condition, half our furniture

was in the home, and the other half was still on the

truck, and the movers were just standing there

waiting on direction from me about what they

needed to do.

   We asked them if they would be willing to

take everything to a storage unit for us. Instead of

saying, *We aren't supposed to do this*, they said,

"Yes we can help you."

   They went back into the house, and loaded

up everything that had been taken inside back onto

the truck. We found a storage facility not too far away, unloaded our furniture, and tipped the men with $120 and lunch for their generosity.

Sigh! In a matter of days, I went from having a plan to get my family settled in, getting the girls enrolled in school, flying back to South Carolina, working another two months, and putting in my resignation, to cancelling our move, putting our things in storage, asking a friend if my daughters and I could stay in a rented room for a few weeks, and making the 13-hour drive back to Columbia with my husband. I had no plan.

The entire way back, I just kept retracing our steps to find out where we went wrong. I asked my husband if he had actually been to the house prior to the day we were due to move. I was looking for someone to blame for this. The plan had failed! I only had a week to get the girls ready for school, and their father was due to leave any day to go back to Iowa for work. Depression began to set in. The feeling of defeat was taking over, and worry and anxiety became my companions.

We were homeless, had no furniture, and my husband was leaving. My seven and eight-year-old daughters needed to go to school, and I needed to make this as easy as possible for them. After my husband left, I had to figure out what we needed to do. I called my sister, who lived about an hour and fifteen minutes away in Charlotte, North Carolina.

As I was explaining everything that had transpired over the last five days, she simply said, "You can stay here. I'll get the girls enrolled in school, and you'll just have to drive back and forth every day until you find something else in the Midwest." Who knew that we would never move out to the Midwest.

I made the drive from Charlotte to Columbia and back, Monday through Friday, from August through December 2011. My daughters shared a bed with my niece, and I slept on the couch. Tired isn't the word for what I was. I was exhausted, sad, and even more depressed. By the time I would get home in the evenings, it was just enough time for me to hug the girls, eat dinner and put them to bed. My sister gave us a place to lay our heads, and didn't ask for one cent from me.

On my morning and evening commutes, I would speak with my husband. We were still looking for a place to stay, right? The seasons were changing, and it was getting colder outside. No biggie, right? Wrong! All of our winter clothes and coats were in that storage unit, 13 hours away. I remember asking if he could go and grab the boxes and send them to Charlotte, so we could have our things before it got too cold. That never happened.

Our communication began to dwindle down to two and three minute conversations and text messages. I called one day in October to ask about the home search, and I was met with resistance. I should have caught the pull away sooner, but I was too consumed with all the other 50 million and eleven things that I had going on. I was in no way prepared for the next stage of our "empty house."

It was time to fly out and get our clothes so we could stay warm in the upcoming winter months. I flew to Iowa, but I didn't ask him to pick me up. I was coming, but not to smile, cuddle, kiss, or even be touched by my spouse. I just wanted our things so we could be warm, and to look this man, my husband, in the face, to see if he was really was looking for another home for all of us to be in together.

Once I got there, he was shocked to say the least. All I wanted was clarity about what was going on with us. The pull away was different this time. There was no sincerity in his voice. His face didn't even look the same. I was beginning to despise him, and what we had become. Before I boarded the plane to head back to Charlotte, we decided that in order for our marriage to truly work, I would have to leave my job and move out there with the girls. I was ready and willing to do whatever was necessary to save my family.

Christmas was quickly approaching, and my husband was flying to Charlotte to be with us as a show of love, sincerity, and support for our family. We were going to all be together again! My sister had just purchased a new home, and welcomed us to continue to stay as long as we needed. She was even looking for jobs for me in Charlotte so I didn't have to keep commuting.

Two days after he got to Charlotte, the honeymoon stage was over. *Two days!* We argued most of the time, and I felt something brewing on the horizon. However, there was something good that came out of him being there...he realized just how much driving I was doing each day, and decided that I needed an apartment back in Columbia.

He found an apartment, we signed the lease, got a few air mattresses, a folding table, groceries, and a few other items. My sister gave me some pots and pans, and my brother who also lives in Charlotte, gave me two old TV's that we could watch in our new apartment.

I could tell my sister wasn't the happiest about the move, but I had to do what was best

> *As a mother, I felt I had failed them, and that hurt more than my marriage falling apart.*

for me and the girls. My youngest daughter was struggling severely in school, and I needed to be able to make time to get her the assistance that she needed. My daughters needed some stability again, and it needed to come from me. As a mother, I felt I had failed them, and that hurt more than my marriage falling apart.

On January 4, 2012, my husband boarded a plane back to the Midwest. He walked down that corridor to his plane, never to return, at least not as my husband. I felt a little more stable now that I had this apartment. My time wouldn't have to be spent driving back and forth every day. My husband and I had decided that once the school year was over for the girls, it would be a better time to move. I just needed to make it to June 2012, right? Wrong!

The next day after he boarded that plane, there was NO communication. I would call and get no answer. I would text and get no reply. He literally didn't answer his own wife. I began to panic at first, but I spoke with his mother, and she had spoken with him, so I knew he was alive. A few days went by, and then he finally answered. His tone was different, and I knew this was the end of our marriage. January 2012 was the longest month ever. Oh, I forgot to mention that I was in grad school while this was all taking place. What a great start to the new year!

During that first month of the new year, in the midst of all the hell unfolding in my life, something great happened! One evening, I walked into class and there was one open seat available at the front. This seat was next to a pastor, but I didn't know this at first.

I sat next to him for about a week, and then one day he leaned over and said, "I'm a Pastor. If you ever need to talk, here is my card."

I took the card and continued on with class. Not many days later, I reached out to him. After speaking with him and his wife, I was able to rest well that night. It had been months since I had a peaceful night's sleep, but I did that night.

Communication was still sparse with my husband, and my daughters were asking where their father was. One of the worst feelings a parent experiences, is not having the answers for their children as it concerns the absent parent. The pain I felt for them was something I never wanted them to experience. Coming from a broken home myself, I understood all too clear the pain of waiting and wanting for your parents. This wasn't supposed to be happening to my daughters. But it was, and it was even more painful to watch.

February 2012 came, and I was invited by the pastor to attend the True Word Church. My daughters and I went, and we have been there ever since. I have grown to know who God is at this church. I developed a relationship with the Father and became a true believer. That open seat the month prior was just God's way of showing me He always had space for me; I just needed to make room for Him.

That year was a bit bumpy in the beginning. Yes, we slept on air mattresses. Yes, we sat on the floor and watched TV. Yes, we only had a few pots and pans. Yes, I cried myself to sleep at night and in the shower. It. Was. Hard. But we had each other. My daughters wanted to know where their daddy was, and I just kept saying at work. One day, I decided that I needed to distract them from what they didn't have. So, I decided to sign them up for cheerleading. I needed their little minds and bodies to stay busy. This also gave me a break from answering questions that I really didn't know the answers to.

By spring, I had sought an attorney for legal counsel, but because I didn't have an address to serve my husband at, it was a waiting game. During this time my sister was coming down to see me and the girls often, and by then, one of my coworkers had given me a king-sized mattress set so the girls and I could get off of the floor. If you've ever slept on an air mattress, then you know that you may start off on an air mattress, but in the morning, you'll wake up on the floor. Anyway, it was during one of those visits that my sister asked, "You do know you have a house full of furniture in storage, right? Do you need money to go get your stuff?"

At that moment it clicked. I did have a house full of furniture, and really nice furniture at that. We didn't need to sleep on the floor any longer.

I made the tough decision to take the money out of my daughters' college funds in order to drive out to Iowa, get a U-Haul truck, load it, and drive it back. Might I add that just a few days before I drove out there, one of my good friends that lived in Iowa called me. She told me how she had just checked the mail, saw a letter from the storage unit, and felt that she needed to open it.

What did that letter say? My furniture was going to be auctioned off that weekend because payment was delinquent $120. Ugh! God was RIGHT ON TIME!

One of my friend's brothers had volunteered to drive out with me, help me load the truck, and drive it back. He even helped me set everything up in the apartment.

Days after arriving back in Columbia, I had just gotten off the phone with my sister, telling her how everything went, and that I was now all set up in the apartment. It was a beautiful Sunday afternoon in June. As I was sitting on the couch in the living room, there was a knock at the door.

Who could this be? I looked through the

peep hole and didn't recognize the young man on

the other side. Maybe he was at the wrong door.

I opened it and he asked, "Are you Onita V.

Brown?"

"Yes," I answered.

He said "You've been

served," and walked away just

as calmly as he came.

He determined th
everything I was
entitled to, I wou
receive!

My heart was racing, I felt a pit in my

stomach. Why am I feeling like this? I knew this

was going to happen. Was I upset that I was served

first, or that I was caught off guard? Or was it the

reality that my marriage was truly over and done

with?

I went back to my lawyer and he began to work on my case. He determined that everything I was entitled to, I would receive! I didn't want anything other than my daughters, so he didn't have to work too hard. My soon to be ex-husband could have the house, I didn't want it anyway. I knew what the prized possessions were, and I had them already.

During this time, I went to church every Sunday, and decided to join. It was the best thing that happened to us. I got my peace back. I became stronger. I was able to sleep without crying. My daughters were thriving. That "empty house" was starting to fill back up, and this time, with the right things that would not be easily taken away.

A year would pass, and only the girls would communicate with their father. To make it easier, I got them their

> *I loved my daughters more than the hatred I felt towards him.*

own cell phone so they could call him any time. He wouldn't need to go through me to speak with them. I wanted to make sure that they maintained a relationship, regardless of what was going on between us. I loved my daughters more than the hatred I felt towards him.

It's now 2013, and D-day was approaching. You know, D-I-V-O-R-C-E. Well like any other young, smart, educated woman would do, I finished my Master of Arts degree in Human Resources and Development. I had started working out, and my body looked better than I expected it to, and my spirit man was strong.

When I walked into that courtroom in October 2013, I was ready! I held my head high, and sat with my shoulders back. I didn't lose anything. I was the real winner. I had my daughters, my dog, and my peace. That was more than enough.

As the years would come in and go out, I continued to focus on my relationship with God and my daughters. We moved to a bigger apartment, and would live there for six years. My Pastor asked me to speak to our church every Sunday and encourage them. Me? Encourage them? Ok.

I've been speaking to them now for over four years, knowing even back then, that this was just preparation for the next stage that God was molding me for.

I decided I needed to fast so I could hear what He was trying to tell me.

I'd even received increase after increase at work, awards, opened a successful business or two, received substantial financial deposits, and traveled with my daughters out of the country.

It wasn't until October 2019, that I would really see how God would reward my obedience. I remember feeling like I was missing something, and I couldn't sleep, or should I say God wouldn't allow me to sleep. So, I decided I needed to fast so I could hear what He was trying to tell me. I kept feeling that I should be looking for a house, and I didn't want that. I wanted a husband first. I had been waiting for over six years and I was ready.

All the houses that I liked were above my $200,000 budget, so this couldn't be what God wanted me to do. He knew my budget so why wasn't I finding what I wanted? I told my realtor that I needed to stop the search for a home because I believe I got ahead of God.

I prayed and asked God if this is what I was supposed to be doing, and if it was, then He needed to find the house, and the finances for this house. About two weeks passed, and I got a text from my realtor saying that she knew of an area that fit what I wanted, but I would have to build.

She set me up with a lender to go over the finances and my credit. We spoke on the phone and of course, I didn't have the credit, but I had the finances. The lender was so reassuring, and had a game plan to get my credit up within the next four months, as my apartment lease was almost up.

Now y'all know God is still in the miracle working business!

I went to the sales office to meet with a representative in order to start the building process. Truth be told, I still didn't want to go, because I wanted to be married first, and I was just told I didn't qualify due to my credit.

I got there and started looking at the neighborhood and thought, *Yea, ok, nobody is listening to me. I'm going to keep my word and go in there, but when the answer is no, oh well.* Now y'all know God is still in the miracle working business! I came out of that meeting with a signed contract that only required $100 down towards my earnest money, $0 for the land, and a $4,500 concession from the builder towards my closing costs. We also set up future payments for the remainder of the earnest money. Let me not forget that I exceeded my budget of $200,000. The amount of the build was actually $319,000, for a five-bedroom, three-full-bath, three-car garage home! I have to be honest...even after all of this, I was still doubtful.

I had 30 days to make modifications to the floor plan, and I was still upset that I was having to do this without a husband. One day, as I was "casting my cares" (some would call it complaining) to the Lord about not being married and having to do this by myself, I clearly heard, "He isn't able to right now." I took that to mean that my husband is enroute, and while he is unable to help me with the plans for our home, I need to act on his behalf. GLORY! There was a shift in the atmosphere! I took God's word seriously, and made the changes necessary for the house. When I went for my meeting with the builder, we started at $319,000. I did not qualify for that amount, but I did qualify for $315,770, and still had everything that I wanted, and that I felt my future spouse would enjoy as well. Let me remind you that my credit score was still not where it needed to be for me to be able to

afford a house this size or this amount. But God!

I was moved up four weeks early for my

preconstruction meeting, and they had acquired

the builder's permit before I had paid all of the

earnest money.

God was

moving! They

started building

> *I heard what she said, but since I knew who was truly in control, I prayed.*

the day after Christmas 2019 without a pre-

approval letter. I decided not to share it with my

daughters until I had the keys in hand.

Fast forward to March 2020. It was time to

pull my credit report to see where I was. I was six

points away. I wasn't discouraged though. My

score literally went up 84 points within four months, so six more points...that's was nothing! I asked my lender if there was anything else I could do to get an even higher score, so that I could get a lower interest rate. She said not at this time, but I could always finance six months later.

Prayer. Changes. Things. I heard what she said, but since I knew who was truly in control, I prayed. I asked God for a higher score so I could have a lower interest rate, which meant lower mortgage payments. On March 13, 2020, my lender ran my credit again, and I not only had more than the six points that I needed, my score was high enough to qualify for the lower interest rate! WON'T HE DO IT?! I received my pre-approval letter March 13, 2020, and closed on our brand-new home March 31, 2020!

After closing, I picked up my daughters and told them we were going house hunting. I was so nervous and excited, and couldn't wait to share with them what the Lord had done for us!

We met the sales rep at the model home, and we were allowed to walk through to see if this was something we might be interested in. They liked it, but wanted to know if there was something available. We drove around the corner, and walked into our home. They loved it! They loved the floors, the layout, the closet space, and even said that our home had everything we'd always said we wanted in a home.

I was about to explode with excitement, when finally, the slide show that I had previously prepared started to play, and they saw me. They were confused as to why I was in these pictures during the building process. My youngest daughter even asked, "Wait, is this our house?" I didn't answer at first. Then I exclaimed, "Just kidding! April fools!" Cruel right? Hold on, it gets better.

So, we are all about to leave, and I opened a drawer in the kitchen where there were two keys. Not just any keys, but the keys they each had picked out the week prior, and that I had cut after closing that very day. I held them in my hands and asked them what they were? The looks on their faces are ones that I'll keep with me forever. My oldest daughter began to cry, and we all embraced in a family hug. We were finally home! It had been

over ten years since we had been in a home that

belonged to us.

REDEMPTION is what I like to equate this

to. Everything that I thought I'd lost, God had

restored with better! This new home was twice the

size of the one that

God is a rewarder of those that diligently seek Him.

we had, and I was

able to do it

without a man, a

husband, a boo, a friend with benefits, or a sugar

daddy. All I needed was to trust, have faith and

believe God would do it. During a pandemic, when

everything was beginning to be shut down, I was

receiving the keys to our home!

God is a rewarder of those that diligently seek Him. I'm a living testimony that He will do exactly what He promised. So, if your struggling, lean on Him and not man. It may not seem like much is changing, but know that He is always working. Some things take longer than others to manifest, but if you hold on to Him, you're in great hands.

People will try to destroy you with lies, and rumors, but

Your testimony is needed for the next to make it.

you have to know who sees it all. He said, "Vengeance is mine, I will repay." Get this...you could never do it how God can. So let Him "empty that house", and He will rebuild it better, stronger and bigger than you could ever imagine. You can't be better and bitter. So, choose better. It's the harder route to take, but also the most rewarding.

You have to decide to take your joy back, your peace back, and your strength back. If they left, let them go, and allow God to redeem everything you thought you lost. Go in peace my beloved. Your testimony is needed for the next to make it.

Connect with Onita

Email: onita_brown@yahoo.com

About The Author

Yashica B. Mack

Yashica Broughton Mack is a Self-Development professional who specializes in working with individuals, as well as entrepreneurs, in developing stronger, more productive relationships.

Yashica believes that understanding your inner-self, and acknowledging the self-talk working inside of you, makes the difference in becoming the better "You".

Yashica is an Army Veteran from Theodore, Alabama, who discovered how to live a PAID in Full Life by coming to terms with, and understanding "Life Happens". Yashica lost her husband, a 23-year Army Veteran, in 2012 from a Neurodegenerative terminal illness, Amyotrophic Lateral Sclerosis (ALS) better known to many as Lou Gehrig's Disease.

Yashica is a graduate of Troy University, obtaining a Bachelor's degree in Psychology, as well as a Master's degree in Counseling and Psychology, a Certified Life Coach, a Certified Les Brown Power Voice Speaker, and an active member of the American Association of Christian Counselors.

Yashica has worked with many professionals in an array of career and personal fields, from professional athletes, other counselors, and military personnel. She has been featured in IMARA Woman Magazine, sports media outlets such as ADSN and World Combat Sports, Kiss FM, local news outlets like WLTX 19, and the 2020 Power Summit with the world's greatest influential motivation speaker, Mr. Les Brown and his team.

Yashica combined her education, training, and experience to become the most sought-after self-development coach, enriching relationships, and managing the eclectic mind across the Americas, and soon the globe.

Yashica is a dedicated mother of three children, committed to living the best version of herself and teaching her children, as well as the world, to do the same.

Her motto is, "You do not have to tear down anyone's kingdom while building your empire. There is plenty of room at the top; it is the bottom that is crowded!"

Read along as Yashica navigates life's obstacles, and becomes a "Why Not Me" mom to give her daughter the help that she needs.

WHY NOT ME?

By

Yashica B. Mack

I understand that forgiveness is not about forgetting. Forgiveness is remembering without anger and rage. Many believe children are gifts. I believe children are a gift to those who pray, prepare, plan, and want them.

At an early age I knew I was different in the way I thought when it came to kids. I really did not want to have any children, and especially, not naturally from my body. After getting older, I decided I wanted to adopt two children.

As a young girl and teenager, growing up Baptist, I was never the one to go look at any babies in church. I did not ooh and ahh over any baby, toddler, or child. It just was not in me. I would stand off to the side as my friends looked on, and played with new babies with such love and excitement. Not me. I seriously looked from a distance.

It was not until I had my first child, a baby girl, that my thought process changed. Funny thing is, I always said, *"I would adopt,"* and God said, *"You will carry and birth your own children out of your body."*

I delivered my daughter on time, but with her own set of issues. Labor was difficult. My body carried the baby perfectly, but when it was time to deliver, my body would not turn her loose. My birthing canal barely opened, and my cervix would not dilate more than a centimeter.

If you are reading this, and have had children, then you understand the pain and agony I was in. My contractions were on top of each other, coming fast and extremely hard.

After failed attempts to make my body dilate, a decision had to be made. You see, a baby in the birthing canal is ready to arrive. My daughter was ready to meet the world, and her mother's body was holding her hostage.

What do most people do when they are feeling locked up with no way out? They panic and some even retreat. That is exactly what my daughter decided to do. She was moving into what the doctors called fetal distress. Fetal distress, according to the American Pregnancy Association, is an emergency in which a baby experiences oxygen deprivation.

I was a young mom, only 20 years old. My mom, my sister, and my husband, were looking on in disbelief, not really knowing what was going on. I do remember the doctor explaining to my husband and mom, that time was of the essence. The baby had to come out, or she could possibly die from a heart attack because she was in distress. She was trying to turn around and go back into my uterus.

The suggestion from the team of doctors, was for me to have an emergency C-section. The response was, "NOW!" The team made a suggestion, and gave an answer as well. Time was not on my side. Time was making the risk of losing her greater.

I vaguely remember the faces in the room. I heard the doctor say, "We need to put the mother to sleep."

Can you imagine that? This is my first child, and I must have a C-section, and be put to sleep. I was in so much pain, and fading, that I do not know who made the decision, my husband or mother. Trust me, at the point of pain that I was experiencing, I did not care. I do remember asking them to please do something.

That was the moment I learned that I have a low tolerance for pain. I was hurting so badly, I could not stay awake. Also, I was not given anything for pain, because my contractions were so close and hard when I arrived at labor and delivery, it was expected that I would be delivering within minutes. We then realized that was not going to be my case.

So much was happening so fast, and yet, it seemed as if I was moving in slow motion outside of my body. I remember seeing myself on the transfer bed, but I saw myself as a spectator, not the actual person lying there with a mask on my face. I do not know how long I was there. I did not have a concept of time.

When I woke up, I did not even know if my baby was alive. I did not hear her cry. I did not see her. I did not see my husband, my mom, or my sister. I was silent and confused. I did not receive her in the birthing room. I had watched enough deliveries on tv shows, and my sister's delivery, to know something was not right. I thought a nurse was supposed to put the baby next to me, and we were supposed to smile and take pictures. None of that happened.

I thought I was alone. Well, I felt very alone, for some odd reason, until moments later, I realized that I was not alone. Minutes seemed like hours before the nurses came and told me I was going to my room.

I asked, "What did I have? A boy or a girl?"

The nurse smiled and said, "A healthy baby girl with a head full of hair."

I was relieved! I'd previously opted not to know the sex before birth. I had a healthy little girl. Wow!

Are you thinking where was everyone, and why was I alone? My family was in the waiting room. I was still on active duty in the Army, stationed in Germany. I returned home to have my child. I was assigned to Keesler Air Force Base. I had my baby in an actual operating room, not a labor and delivery room. Therefore, standard operating procedures were enforced to include only staff in the operating room.

After delivery, I was moved to the recovery room. Time did pass; I just did not realize how much because I was sedated with anesthesia. My daughter was in the infant room with her father, who held her first. He was able to put her on his chest FIRST. She heard his heartbeat outside the body FIRST, not MINE!

When this collaboration was written and published, my daughter was 25. Many changes happened between that day in September 1995 and the writing of this chapter. My daughter's father and I divorced when my daughter was three years old. I remained affiliated with the military, and had multiple missions that took me away from her. I did marry again, and added two boys to our family. In 2012, my husband passed away. Not only did I lose a husband, but my daughter, who was 16 at the time, lost the father she claimed.

After my husband passed away, the relationship between my daughter and I turned sour. We loved each other as mother and daughter, but we did not seem to like one another. About two months after my husband's passing, we had an argument, and my daughter just walked out of the house and left home. She just walked out as I was still talking to her.

Now, I am a black momma, and if you are reading closely, any momma can probably relate to how my blood was boiling at that moment. That is something we just do not tolerate. However, I did. You see, I was a cross between a traditional black momma raised in the south, and a modern young momma being understanding, and somewhat detached myself. However, this girl was gone for a couple of days without a phone call, text, or letter. When she returned, I said nothing. I do not know what thoughts I was having, as complicated as this situation was, but I said nothing, and my daughter did not say anything either. She came back and carried on as if she was not just gone for three days.

This defiant behavior continued, but the disappearing did not show up again until two years later. She was a college student living in South Carolina. I eventually moved back to South Carolina as well, because I wanted to be close to her, and back to the place my husband and I loved so much. While we were in separate states, our relationship was that of a mother and daughter. She missed me and I missed her. Once I moved to South Carolina with her brothers, the relationship went sour again.

Over the course of about two years, she would stay with me, get mad, and just disappear again. Later, during her time away, she would call and ask me to come get her, or to send for her. This was happening a lot, until one day, I just told her no more. I suggested she stay on the other side of the door, because this behavior was not welcomed, and it was such a bad influence on my younger sons. Although I said this, I still allowed her to come and leave again. My boundaries were not clear.

I was convinced she was on drugs. What else could explain this behavior? Also, she just did not like me, and I did not like her. Those were my thoughts and that is what I believed. I settled with that thought because from birth, she and I missed the bonding. She bonded with her father. I convinced myself that she was not connected to me, and I was not connected to her. This was easy. I was okay with knowing every mother-daughter relationship is not like Claire Huxtable, Denise, and Sondra. I was just fine then. I was comfortable seeing and experiencing the changes leading to the truth. My perceived truth.

The pandemic of 2020 ravaged the country, forcing us to stay in; Forcing us to see underlying issues within ourselves and our families. The quarantine forced us to examine our priorities, and what we were tagging as important in our lives. I learned a lot in 2020. We made progress this time in understanding the issues between us.

It was March 1, 2020. Tensions were high in my house. My daughter, with her shenanigans as I called them, left again, but this time was different. This time had darkness over it. This time I cared. I placed that dreadful call to 9-1-1 and reported a missing person. The detectives came out and took my statement, gathering information such as her name, height, weight, hair color, a picture, etc. I gave it all to them. I was assured they would do the best they could to find her.

The police officers were not gone from my home ten minutes, before I received a phone call that would again change my life forever. My son was in a solo car accident in Fairfield County, and was being transported to Richland County Trauma Hospital. That was the first time in my life I broke down.

For a moment, my heart stopped beating, and my chest could not rise. I lost control of the situation. I lost two children in the same night within minutes of each other. I had my 11-year-old holding me as I could only cry and moan. The little one knew something serious was happening, because he had never seen his rock like this.

Phone calls were made from afar, and Angels showed up. As I write this, the memories come, and the blanks are still blank. All my life, I knew I was strong, and had endured a great deal. I asked God, *"Was I being prepped for this moment?"* I did not ask Him, *"Why me?"* I asked Him, *"Why not me?"* I knew as long as it is me, then someone else would be spared.

With all the challenges in my life, I asked God the same thing, but this time, I asked for more strength. I needed it for my 11-year-old that I had to leave home, and confused. I was traveling to the hospital with Angels, and other Angels were dispatched, and beat us to the hospital. This is important, because I did not call and activate these Angels. God assigned the mission to someone else. Remember, I was crying and moaning, as an 11-year-old held me.

I am moving quickly through the story, and as you read, you are probably asking where is my youngest son? Was my daughter found? Did my oldest son survive the accident? My youngest son was taken by yet another Angel to be comforted at her home, and yes, my oldest son lived through the accident. He sustained many broken bones, and yet recovered completely!

This chapter is about my daughter. Yes, she was found that night. Shortly after, my daughter was hospitalized. In the course of her hospitalization on the mental health floor, I received good news. My daughter was diagnosed with a mental illness. All these years she battled this without knowing what was going on inside her head. Her behavior resulted from us not knowing. I chopped it up to her being a defiant teenager that hated her mother, who became a young adult that hated her mother. None of that was true. Had we caught the disorder early, this chapter would definitely read differently.

Think about this quote by Les Brown, *"When life knocks you down, try to land on your back, because if you can look up, you can get up."* From my life's journey I would say, *"Once you get up do something different."* That is what I must do… "something different". I must retrain my thoughts, and forgive the memories of the defiant teenager turned young adult, and see her again as my loving daughter that fell and got up. Now she knows something different.

We look and live in this life, and oftentimes, what we see is not the reality. We, and I, am guilty of not knowing what mental illness looks like, because I believed and knew all the signs of drug abuse first. I challenge you, the reader, that as society and schools teach us all about drugs and addictive behavior, that you, the reader, take it upon yourself, to learn and be knowledgeable of what mental illness looks like. I think about my daughter and how it must have been for her being trapped inside for all those years with nowhere to retreat. She could not bring herself out.

There is a continuation of how to retrain your brain and behaviors when mental illness shows up. Not only do I have to learn to adjust and forgive, but so do other family members. My daughter must learn to forgive herself. She must learn her worth. That is a process, but a process worth going through. My daughter deserves a peaceful life, and God gave her a "Why Not Me" mom to help her.

Connect with Yashica

Instagram: https://www.instagram.com/yashicab4u

Facebook: https://www.facebook.com/yashicaB4U

LinkedIn: https://www.linkedin.com/in/yashica-mack-a400928b

Twitter: https://www.twitter.com/Yashica95

Website: www.YashicaB.com

~ References ~

Flourish

- https://www.cdc.gov/violenceprevention/aces/fastfact.html
- www.mayoclinic.org (tween and seen health)

- 1-800-672-2296

Unmasking to Empower

- Vagianos, Alanna. (2017, December 07) "30 Shocking Domestic Violence Statistics That Remind Us It's An Epidemic." *Huffpost,* 23 Oct. 2014, huffpost.com/entry/domestic-violence-statistics_n_5959776. Accessed 24 Dec. 2020.
- For anonymous, confidential help, 24/7, please call the National Domestic Violence Hotline at 1-800-799-7233 (SAFE) or 1-800-787-3224 (TTY).

Silver Spoon

- Savita V. Carothers LMFT - Thousand Oaks, CA | CareDash
  https://www.caredash.com/doctors/savita-carothers-wjlp9
- Business: Self Revelations Counseling Services
  Owner/Provider: Danita Davis LCSW (Licensed Clinical Social Worker)
  Address: 1711 East Central Texas Expressway, Ste 108-6, Killeen, Texas 76541
  Phone 254-833-5141
  Fax: 254-833-5143
  Email:danitadavis@gmail.com